불교영어

중급·2

불교영어
Buddhist English
중급·2

대한불교조계종 교육원 불학연구소 편찬

조계종
출판사

일러두기

- 본서의 영문본은 한글본과 일대일 대칭의 번역이 아닙니다.
- 일부 불교 용어 및 문장은 독자의 이해를 돕기 위해 완곡하게 표현하거나 부분적으로 표현하였습니다.
- 《불교영어중급2》의 Part1과 〈영어 단어장〉은 mp3 파일로 제작되었습니다.
  파일은 대한불교조계종 홈페이지(http://www.buddhism.or.kr/) 상단 메뉴 '종무행정 〉 종무자료실 〉 승가교육'에서 다운 받으실 수 있습니다.

≫ 책을 펴내며

    본 연구소에서는 2012년 ≪불교영어초급 1·2≫을 발간한데 이어, 금년 3월에 ≪불교영어중급 1·2≫를 펴내게 되었습니다. 이번에는 특히 불교영어를 접하시는 분들의 단어 암기에 대한 어려움을 고려해 각 장의 중요 어휘들을 모아 〈영어 단어장〉도 함께 발간하게 되었습니다.
    이 책의 내용과 주요 구성은 기존의 ≪불교영어초급 1·2≫와 동일하게 세 부분으로 구분하여 1부에서는 〈영어 회화〉, 2부에서는 〈불교 교리〉, 3부에서는 〈한국불교의 역사와 문화〉를 다루었으며, 각 본문 사이의 '쉬어가는 코너'에서는 여러 선사들의 선시 등을 수록하였습니다.
    1부 〈영어 회화〉편에서는 7개의 장으로 나누어져 있으며, 최대한 대화의 형식을 취하고자 노력하였습니다. 각 장의 주요내용으로는 템플스테이, 사찰 안내, 전화 대화, 사찰 생활, 연등 축제, 출가와 해탈, 스님이 외국인에게 지켜야 할 예절 등을 다루고 있습니다.
    2부 〈불교 교리와 수행〉편에서는 3개의 장으로 나누어져 있으며, ≪불교영어초급 1·2≫에 수록된 〈불교 교리〉편의 어휘들보다 심화된 어휘들로 내용을 구성하였습니다. 각 장의 주요내용으로는 불교의 윤리, 경전과 어록의 가르침, 한국의 선수행 등을 다루고 있으며, 3부 〈한국불교의 의례〉편에서는 사찰 의례, 천도재, 한국의 고승 등을 다루고 있습니다.
    이 책은 주로 승가대학 스님들의 교재로 활용되기에 대화의 주제와 내용들이 스님들 중심으로 엮어져 있는 것이 특징이기도 합니다. 사찰 승가대학 스님들뿐만 아니라 일반 불자님들도 영어로 한국불교를 소개하고 포교하는 데 많은 도움이 되기를 기대합니다.
    본문에 게재된 사진과 그림들은 대한불교조계종 불교문화사업단에서 도움을 받았습니다.
    좋은 책이 나오도록 많은 관심과 배려를 보여 주신 관계자 분들께 깊은 감사를 드립니다.

2558(2014)년 3월
대한불교조계종 교육원 불학연구소

≫ Structures

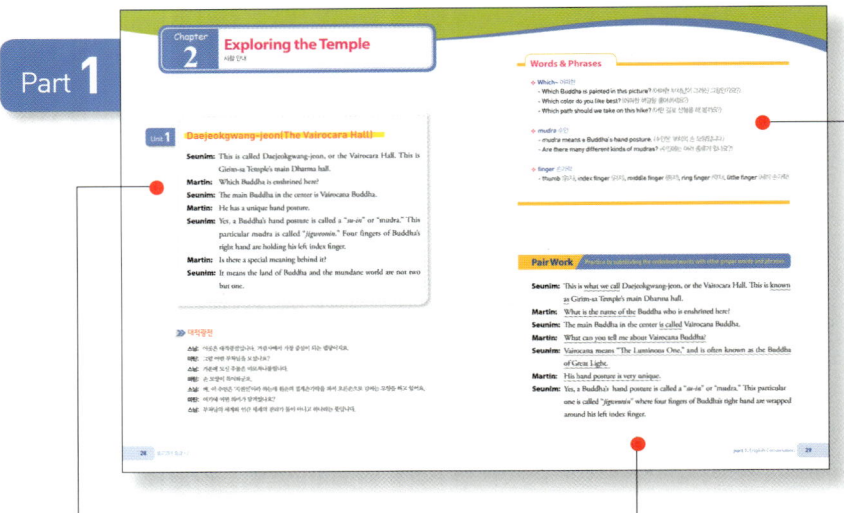

Words and Phrases 문법 정리와 어휘 활용법

본문과 관련된 내용의 문법을 한 번 더 정리하면서 그와 관련된 다양한 표현의 회화를 익히도록 했습니다. 핵심 문법 패턴을 외워 여러 상황의 단어를 활용해보면 자연스러운 대화가 완성될 것입니다.

Unit

1부 〈영어 회화〉 편은 스님들이 사찰에서 일상적으로 가장 많이 접하는 주제를 7개의 장으로 나누고 각 장마다 가능한 대화 상황을 7단원으로 수록하였습니다. 7개의 주제는 템플스테이, 사찰 안내, 전화 대화, 사찰 생활, 연등 축제, 출가와 해탈, 스님이 외국인에게 지켜야 할 예절입니다.

Pair Work 말하기

한글 회화와 영어 회화, 그 단원에 쓰인 단어와 구문의 해설, 그리고 파트너와 함께 관련 회화를 더 연습할 수 있는 'pair work'입니다. 단어와 구문의 경우 되도록 스님들의 환경에 맞는 것으로 수록하여 더욱 효과적인 학습을 기하였습니다. 'pair work'에서는 밑줄 친 부분을 다른 단어로 대체하여 동일한 문장을 지루함 없이 자연스럽게 암기가 가능하도록 하였습니다.

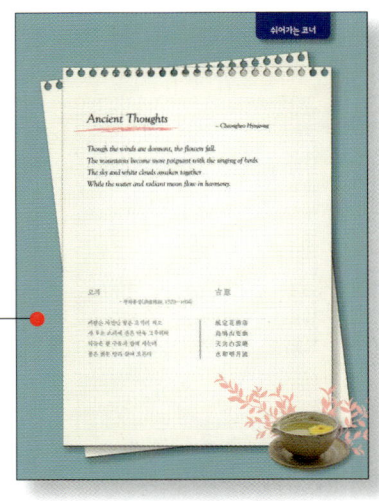

쉬어가는 코너

한숨 돌리고 머리를 식히며 불교문학과 만나는 공간입니다. 아름다운 찬불가와 마음속 깊은 여운을 남기는 선시를 감상하는 공간으로 잠시 휴식을 취하도록 하였습니다.

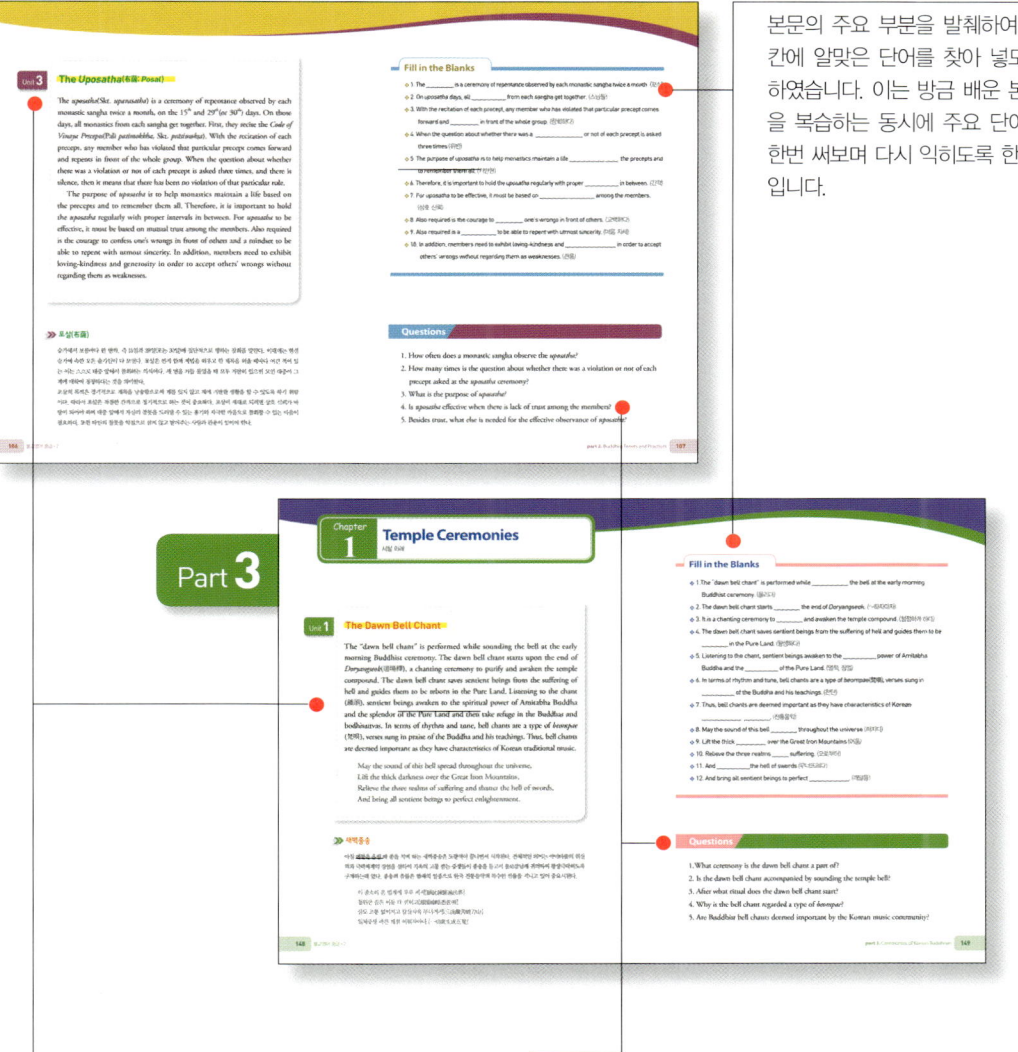

Fill in the Blanks
빈칸 넣기

본문의 주요 부분을 발췌하여 빈칸에 알맞은 단어를 찾아 넣도록 하였습니다. 이는 방금 배운 본문을 복습하는 동시에 주요 단어를 한번 써보며 다시 익히도록 한 것입니다.

Unit 각 주제에 해당하는 설명

2부 〈불교 교리와 수행〉과 3부 〈한국 불교의 의례〉에서는 기본적으로 알아야 할 주제를 선정하여 먼저 한글 지문, 그에 해당하는 영어 지문을 실었습니다.

Questions 질문

본문에서 배운 내용에 대한 질문을 주고받는 상황입니다. 이 부분은 학생들끼리 연습해도 되고 선생님과 학생이 질문을 주고받아도 됩니다. 핵심 패턴을 익혀 그 의미를 확실하게 전달할 수 있도록 하세요.

≫ Content

책을 펴내며   005

이 책의 구성   006

Part 1
English Conversation 영어회화

Chapter 1. Templestay 템플스테이
- **Unit 1.** How to Walk in Temples 경내에서 걷기   014
- **Unit 2.** Greetings 인사   017
- **Unit 3.** Managing Shoes 신발 관리   019
- **Unit 4.** Etiquette in the Dharma Hall 법당 예절   022
- **Unit 5.** Using Chairs 의자 사용   024

Chapter 2. Exploring the Temple 사찰 안내
- **Unit 1.** Daejeokgwang-jeon (The Virocana Hall) 대적광전   028
- **Unit 2.** Gwaneun-jeon (The Avalokitesvara Hall) 관음전   030
- **Unit 3.** Mita-jeon (The Amitabha Hall) 미타전   032
- **Unit 4.** Jijang-jeon (The Ksitigarbha Hall) 지장전   034
- **Unit 5.** Josa-jeon (The Hall of Patriarchs) 조사전   036

Chapter 3. Conversation over the Phone 전화 대화
- **Unit 1.** Inquiring about the Templestay Program   038
  템플스테이 프로그램 문의
- **Unit 2.** Inquiring about the Temple's Facility 템플스테이 시설 문의   041
- **Unit 3.** Inquiring about Meals during a Templestay Program   043
  템플스테이 식사 문의
- **Unit 4.** Bedtime at a Templestay Program 템플스테이 취침 시간   045
- **Unit 5.** Suggesting a Templestay to a Friend 템플스테이 권유   047

Chapter 4. The Temple Life 사찰 생활

Unit 1. Importance of Being Punctual 시간 지키기 — 050
Unit 2. Meal Etiquette 공양 예절 — 052
Unit 3. Shoe Etiquette 신발 관리 — 054
Unit 4. *Anhaeng* (Walking in a Single Line) 안행 — 056
Unit 5. *Hapjang Banbae* (Pressing One's Palms Together and Making a Half-Bow) 합장 반배 — 058

Chapter 5. Lotus Lantern Festival 연등 축제

Unit 1. The Origin of the Lotus Lantern Festival 연등 축제의 유래 — 062
Unit 2. Intangible Cultural Asset 무형문화재 — 065
Unit 3. Visiting the Traditional Lantern Exhibit 전통 등 전시회 관람 — 067
Unit 4. Watching the Lotus Lantern Parade 연등 행렬 관람 — 069
Unit 5. Buddha's Birthday Celebration Ceremony 봉축법요식 — 072

Chapter 6. Ordination and Enlightenment 출가와 해탈

Unit 1. Getting Ordained as a Buddhist Monk 출가 — 074
Unit 2. The Life of a *Haengja* (Apprentice) 행자 생활 — 076
Unit 3. Monastic College (Sangha College) 승가 대학 — 079
Unit 4. Buddhist Practice as a Seunim 수행 — 081
Unit 5. Liberation 해탈 — 083

Chapter 7. Etiquette with Foreign Participants for Seunims to Remember 스님이 외국인에게 지켜야 할 예절

Unit 1. How to Address Westerners on a First-Name Base 이름 부르기 — 086
Unit 2. Introducing Oneself 자기소개 — 088
Unit 3. Accommodating Participants' Needs during Meditation 좌선에 대한 배려 — 090
Unit 4. Respecting Each Individual's Decisions 선택의 문제 — 092
Unit 5. Acceptance 포용성 — 094

Part 2
Buddhist Tenets and Practices
불교 교리와 수행

Chapter 1. The Ethics of Buddhism 불교의 윤리

Unit 1. Ten Unwholesome Deeds 십악업 — 100
Unit 2. *The Verse of the Common Teaching of the Seven Buddhas* — 103
칠불통계
Unit 3. The *Uposatha* 포살 — 106
Unit 4. The *Pavāraṇā* 자자 — 108
Unit 5. Repentance 참회 — 110
Unit 6. The Three Refuges, the Five Precepts, the Ten Precepts, — 112
and the Precepts for Bhikkhus and Bhikkhunis
삼귀의계, 오계, 십계, 비구・비구니계

Chapter 2. The Teachings from the Scriptures and the Recorded Sayings of Sages 경전과 어록의 가르침

Unit 1. The *Heart Sutra* 반야심경 — 116
Unit 2. The *Diamond Sutra* 금강경 — 119
Unit 3. *Verses on the Mind of Faith* 신심명 — 123
Unit 4. *Song of Enlightenment* 증도가 — 126
Unit 5. The *Mirror of Seon* 선가귀감 — 129

Chapter 3. Seon Practice in Korea 한국의 선수행

Unit 1. *Instructions for Sitting Seon* 좌선의 — 132
Unit 2. Practice of Ganhwa Seon 간화선 수행 — 136
    2.1 The Three Essentials of Ganhwa Seon 간화선의 세 가지 중요한 요점
    2.2 *Hwadu* and *Gongan* 화두, 공안
    2.3 Implementation of *Manhaeng* and Seon Practice
        만행의 실천과 선수행

Part 3
Ceremonies of Korean Buddhism
한국불교의 의례

Chapter 1. Temple Ceremonies 사찰의례
Unit 1. The Dawn Bell Chant 새벽종송 — 148
Unit 2. *Yebul*, Morning and Evening Buddhist Ceremonies 예불 — 150
Unit 3. The Evening Bell Chant 저녁종송 — 155

Chapter 2. Cheondo-jae 천도재
Unit 1. *Sasipgu-jae*, the Forty-Nine Day Ceremony 49재 — 158
Unit 2. *Suryuk-jae*, the Water-Land Ceremony 수륙재 — 162
Unit 3. *Yeongsan-jae* 영산재 — 165
Unit 4. *Yesu-jae* 예수재 — 168

Chapter 3. Eminent Monks of Korea 한국의 고승
Unit 1. Wonhyo 원효 — 172
Unit 2. Uisang 의상 — 176
Unit 3. Jinul 지눌 — 182
Unit 4. Iryeon 일연 — 186
Unit 5. Taego Bou 태고보우 — 190
Unit 6. Seosan Hyujeong 서산휴정 — 194
Unit 7. Gyeongheo Seongu 경허성우 — 199
Unit 8. Manhae 만해 — 203
Unit 9. Toe-ong Seongcheol 퇴옹성철 — 208

Appendix : Answers
문제 해답 — 212

Part 1

English Conversation
영어 회화

- Chapter 1 **Templestay** 템플스테이
- Chapter 2 **Exploring the Temple** 사찰 안내
- Chapter 3 **Conversation over the Phone** 전화 대화
- Chapter 4 **The Temple Life** 사찰 생활
- Chapter 5 **Lotus Lantern Festival** 연등 축제
- Chapter 6 **Ordination and Enlightenment** 출가와 해탈
- Chapter 7 **Etiquette with Foreign Participants for Seunims to Remember** 스님이 외국인에게 지켜야 할 예절

Chapter 1 **Templestay**
템플스테이

Unit 1 How to Walk in Temples

Seunim: When you walk in temples, please walk slowly and quietly.
Martin: Is running not allowed?
Seunim: No, I am afraid it is against temple etiquette.
Martin: Is it okay to talk while walking?
Seunim: Yes. However, please keep your voice low because it is important to be mindful even when you are walking.

≫ 경내에서 걷기

스님: 경내를 걸을 때는 천천히 침착하게 걷습니다.
마틴: 뛰면 안 되나요?
스님: 안되지요. 사찰 예절에 어긋납니다.
마틴: 그럼 걸으면서 이야기를 나누는 것은 괜찮지요?
스님: 예, 하지만 되도록 조용히 대화하십시오. 걸을 때도 마음을 챙기는 것이 중요합니다.

Words & Phrases

❖ **Is _____ not allowed?** ~안 되나요?
- Is music not allowed? (음악을 틀면 안 되나요?)
- Is talking not allowed? (말을 하면 안 되나요?)
- Is eating snacks not allowed? (간식을 먹으면 안 되나요?)
- Is using cell phones not allowed? (핸드폰을 사용하면 안 되나요?)
- Is wearing perfume not allowed? (향수를 쓰면 안 되나요?)

❖ **I am afraid** 반대 의견을 정중히 제시하는 표현
- I am afraid I cannot agree. (유감스럽지만 동의할 수 없습니다.)
- I am afraid that is not allowed. (안타깝지만 허락되지 않습니다.)
- I am afraid that is not possible. (죄송하지만 가능하지 않습니다.)

❖ **It is against ~** ~에 어긋납니다
- It is against our policy. (규칙에 어긋납니다.)
- It is against my religious beliefs. (저의 종교적 믿음에 어긋나는 일입니다.)
- It is against our reservation rules. (저희 예약 규칙에 어긋나는 일입니다.)

❖ **while ~** ~하는 동안
- Please take pictures while you look around. (구경하는 동안 사진을 찍으세요.)
- While you are participating in this program, do not use your cell phone. (참여하는 동안 핸드폰은 사용하지 마세요.)
- Please form a single line while you are waiting. (기다리는 동안 줄을 서 주세요.)

❖ **be mindful** 마음을 챙기다
- Please be mindful while you eat. (식사하는 동안 마음을 챙기세요.)
- Let's be mindful every moment of our lives. (삶의 매 순간 마음을 챙깁시다.)

Pair Work

Practice by substituting the underlined words with other proper words and phrases.

Seunim: Please walk slowly and carefully while you walk around temples.

Martin: Am I not allowed to run?

Seunim: No, temple etiquette does not allow it.

Martin: How about the trails around the temple grounds? Am I not allowed to run there either?

Seunim: No, I am afraid not. It is important to remain mindful, so walk slowly and quietly at all times. Also, it may not be safe.

Unit 2 Greetings

Seunim: There are many seunims who live in the temple.
When you see them, please greet them by offering a half bow with your palms together.
Anna: Is that temple etiquette?
Seunim: Yes. In Buddhism, seunims are revered and respected as teachers from whom lay people learn the Buddha-dharma.
Anna: I see. So, a half bow is a way of paying respect.
Seunim: Exactly. Put your palms together in front of your chest and take a half bow.

》 인사

스님: 이 절에는 여러 스님이 계십니다.
경내에서 스님을 만나면 합장 반배를 하시기 바랍니다.
애나: 그게 사찰 예절인가요?
스님: 불교에서 스님은 공경의 대상이자 재가자에게 불법을 가르치는 스승이기 때문입니다.
애나: 그러니까 공경의 표시로 반배를 올리는 거군요.
스님: 그렇지요. 두 손을 가슴 앞에 모으고 허리를 공손히 숙여 인사하면 됩니다.

Words & Phrases

❖ **by + 동사** 어떠한 방식으로 행동을 취하다
 - Pay respect by prostrating oneself. (절을 하여 예의를 갖추다.)
 - Follow rules by being punctual. (시간을 지켜 규칙을 따르다.)
 - Focus on practice by being mindful. (마음을 챙겨 수련에 집중하다.)
 - Enjoy nature by going hiking. (산행에 참여해 자연을 느끼다.)

❖ **a way of ~** 표시
 - It is a way of showing gratitude. (감사의 표시)
 - It is a way of displaying affection. (호감의 표시)

❖ **Is this/that ~?** ~인가요?
 - Is that the dormitory? (저기가 숙소인가요?)
 - Is this your luggage? (이것이 당신의 짐입니까?)
 - Is this the kitchen? (여기가 주방인가요?)

❖ **lay people** 재가자
 - Lay people supports Buddhism while making a living in a secular world.
   (재가자는 속세에서 생계를 유지하며 불교를 지원합니다.)

❖ **Buddha-dharma** 불법

Pair Work
Practice by substituting the underlined words with other proper words and phrases.

Seunim: There are a <u>great number of</u> seunims who <u>reside</u> in the temple. When you <u>meet</u> them, <u>please pay respect</u> with a half bow while putting your palms together.

Anna: <u>Would it be part of</u> temple etiquette?

Seunim: Yes. In Buddhism, seunims are <u>recognized and respected</u> as teachers from whom lay people learn the Buddha-dharma.

Anna: I see. So, a half bow <u>expresses respect for them.</u>

Seunim: Yes. <u>Gather your palms together</u> in front of your chest and take a half-bow.

Unit 3

Managing Shoes

Seunim: Anna, you have come to experience monastic life for two days, right?

Anna: Yes, for one night and two days.

Seunim: Wonderful. If so, there are some basic manners we ask you to follow.

Anna: Yes, please explain them for me.

Seunim: First, please take off your shoes before entering all buildings and rooms.

Anna: Okay, I am well aware of that.

Seunim: After you take off your shoes, make sure the shoes are tidily arranged in front of the door.

Anna: Is there a reason behind that?

Seunim: It is to be mindful of oneself and maintain calmness at all times. In the Buddhist tradition, we call this "watching each and every step carefully."

▶▶ 신발 관리

스님: 애나는 이틀 동안 스님들의 생활을 체험하러 오셨습니다. 맞지요?

애나: 예, 1박 2일 동안이요.

스님: 그렇다면 애나가 지켜 주셔야 할 예절이 있습니다.

애나: 예, 말씀해 주세요.

스님: 우선 경내 모든 전각과 방에 들어갈 때는 신발을 벗습니다.

애나: 예, 그건 잘 알고 있습니다.

스님: 신발을 벗은 후엔 가지런히 정돈해 놓고 방에 들어갑니다.

애나: 그건 왜죠?

스님: 늘 고요하게 자신을 돌아보고 침착한 마음을 간직하기 위해서 입니다. 불교의 전통에서는 이를 일러 '조고각하(照顧脚下)'라고 합니다.

Words & Phrases

❖ **come to + 동사** ~하러 오다
- I came to enjoy Korea's traditional culture. (한국의 전통 문화를 즐기러 왔습니다.)
- I came to release stress. (스트레스를 날려 버리고자 왔습니다.)
- I came to immerse myself in peace. (평화로움을 만끽하고자 왔습니다.)

❖ **There is (are) ~** ~이 있습니다
- There are many legends about this place. (이곳에는 많은 전설이 전해지고 있습니다.)
- There are many Buddhist temples in Korea. (한국에는 많은 사찰들이 있습니다.)
- There isn't any news so far. (아직은 소식이 없습니다.)

❖ **be aware of / be familiar with / know** 알고 있다
- She is well aware of this area. (그녀는 이 지역을 잘 알고 있습니다.)
- Is he aware that mountains can be dangerous? (그는 산속이 위험하다는 것을 알고 있나요?)
- It's important to be aware of one's own mind. (자기 자신의 마음을 잘 아는 것이 중요합니다.)
- I am familiar with temple etiquette. (저는 사찰 예절을 잘 알고 있습니다.)
- I am familiar with the history of the Jogye Order of Korean Buddhism.
  (조계종의 역사에 대해 알고 있습니다.)

❖ **explain~ in detail** 자세히 설명하다
- Would you explain it in detail? (자세히 설명해 주시겠어요?)
- Please explain the accident in detail to me. (나에게 그 사건을 자세히 설명해 주세요.)

❖ **take off / remove** 벗다
- Take off your coat. (코트 벗으세요.)
- You should take off your shoes before entering rooms in Korea.
  (한국에서는 방에 들어가기 전에 신발을 벗어야 한다.)

Pair Work
Practice by substituting the underlined words with other proper words and phrases.

Seunim: Anna, you wanted to experience temple life for two days, right?

Anna: Yes, for one night and two days.

Seunim: Wonderful. If that's the case, we have some basic manners we ask you to follow.

Anna: Yes, please elaborate on them for me.

Seunim: First, please remove your shoes before entering all buildings and rooms.

Anna: Okay, is there anything else I should be aware of?

Seunim: After you remove your shoes, make sure your shoes are neatly arranged in front of the door.

Anna: What's the reason behind that?

Seunim: We strive to be mindful of ourselves and retain calmness at all times. In the Buddhist tradition, this is known as "watching each and every step carefully."

Unit 4

Etiquette in the Dharma Hall

Seunim: When you enter the Dharma hall, please use the side entrances on the left or right.

Anna: How about the entrance in the center?

Seunim: Good question! The entrance in the center is called "*eoganmun*" and reserved for seunims only. Please remember to take your shoes off and arrange them tidily in front of the door.

Anna: As soon as I enter, I must do a half bow, right?

Seunim: Yes, very good. Then, grab a meditation cushion and place it where you wish to sit. Offer three prostrations to Buddha and have a seat on the cushion.

▶▶ 법당 예절

스님: 법당에 들어갈 때는 오른쪽이나 왼쪽 문을 이용합니다.

애나: 가운데 문은 안 되나요?

스님: 어간문은 스님만 사용할 수 있습니다. 신발은 가지런히 벗고 들어갑니다.

애나: 들어가자마자 합장 반배를 하는 거지요?

스님: 예, 그런 다음, 법당 한 편에 쌓여 있는 좌복 중 하나를 가지고 와서 앉을 자리에 놓습니다. 그리고 부처님께 삼배를 올린 후 자리에 앉습니다.

Words & Phrases

❖ **when+ (주어) + 동사 ~할 때는**
  - When you meditate, try to let go of your thoughts. (참선을 할 때는 생각을 내려놓아야 합니다.)
  - When you enter the Dharma hall, please avoid speaking loudly.
    (법당에 들어오면 큰 소리는 자제해야 합니다.)
  - When you place your meditation cushion down, do it quietly while being mindful.
    (좌복을 내려놓을 때는 마음을 챙기며 조용히 놓습니다.)

❖ **as soon as ~ ~하자마자, ~하자 곧**
  - The weather cleared up as soon as we arrived. (우리가 도착하자마자 날씨가 개었습니다.)
  - As soon as I arrived at the temple, I felt very peaceful.
    (절에 도착하자마자 마음이 평화로워졌습니다.)
  - Your daily schedule will start as soon as you wake up in the morning.
    (아침에 일어나자마자 일정이 시작될 겁니다.)
  - Please email me your response as soon as you can! (답변을 주실 수 있을 때, 곧바로 이메일 주세요!)

❖ **main entrance** 정문, 중앙 출입구 / **side entrance** 옆문, 측면 출입구

❖ **prostration / prostrate / bow** 바닥에 엎드려 하는 절, 절하다

Pair Work
Practice by substituting the underlined words with other proper words and phrases.

Seunim: When you enter the Dharma hall, please <u>enter through</u> the side entrances on the left or right.

Anna: <u>What is the door in the center used for?</u>

Seunim: Good question! The entrance in the center is called "*eoganmun*" and <u>it is for seunims only</u>.

Anna: As soon as I enter, I should <u>prostrate myself</u>, right?

Seunim: <u>No, I am afraid not. First, you should do a half bow</u>, then <u>get</u> a meditation cushion and <u>put</u> it where you <u>want to be seated</u>. It is only then you offer three prostrations to Buddha and <u>sit down</u>.

Unit 5

Using Chairs

Jackson: Seunim, when I meditate, do I have to sit in a lotus position?

Seunim: Is it difficult for you to sit on the floor?

Jackson: Yes, I can do it only for a short period of time.

Seunim: If that is the case, please feel free to sit on the chair located in the back of the Dharma hall.

Jackson: Would that be OK?

Seunim: Of course, focusing your mind is far more important than your physical posture.

의자 사용

잭슨: 스님, 참선을 할 때는 꼭 가부좌를 하고 앉아야 하나요?

스님: 잭슨은 가부좌가 어려우시군요.

잭슨: 예, 잠시라면 몰라도 오랫동안은 힘듭니다.

스님: 그렇다면 법당 뒤에 놓여 있는 의자를 사용하세요.

잭슨: 그래도 괜찮아요?

스님: 예, 자세보다 중요한 것은 마음의 집중이니까요.

Words & Phrases

❖ **lotus position** 가부좌 / **full lotus position** 결가부좌 / **half lotus position** 반가부좌

❖ **Is it difficult? / Is it challenging? / Is it hard?** 어려우신가요?
- Is it challenging for you to go hiking? (산행을 하기가 어려우신가요?)
- Is it difficult for you to follow the program agenda? (일정을 소화하기가 어려우신가요?)
- Is it hard for you to eat Korean food? (한국 음식을 먹는 것이 어려우신가요?)

❖ **for a short period of time** 잠시 동안
- We will take a break for a short period of time. (잠시 동안 휴식을 취하겠습니다.)

❖ **If that is the case / In that case** 그렇다면
- If that's the case, you can choose which program to attend.
  (그렇다면 일정 중 원하시는 것만 참여하시면 됩니다.)
- If that's the case, I will switch your reservation to next week.
  (그렇다면 다음 주로 예약을 바꿔 드리겠습니다.)

❖ **feel free to ~** ~하셔도 됩니다
- Please feel free to share your own opinions. (자신의 의견을 제시하셔도 됩니다.)
- Feel free to enjoy the beautiful scenery! (경치를 맘껏 즐기셔도 됩니다!)
- Feel free to use your free time. (자유 시간을 누리셔도 됩니다.)
- Feel free to ask any questions. (질문을 하셔도 됩니다.)
- Feel free to ask questions after the Dharma talk. (법문이 끝나고 질문을 하셔도 됩니다.)

❖ **It is far more important to~** 더욱 중요합니다
- It is far more important for you to find inner peace than to feel stressed.
  (스트레스를 받는 것보다 평화로운 마음을 갖는 것이 더욱 중요합니다.)
- It is far more important to focus on inner beauty than to see fancy exteriors.
  (화려함을 중요시하는 것보다 내면을 보는 것이 더욱 중요합니다.)

Pair Work

Practice by substituting the underlined words with other proper words and phrases.

Jackson: Seunim, when I meditate, am I required to sit in a lotus position?

Seunim: Is it challenging for you to sit in a full lotus position? Then, how about the half lotus position?

Jackson: Simply sitting on the floor is already a challenge for me. I can only do it for a short while.

Seunim: If that is the case, please go ahead and sit on the chair located in the back of the Dharma hall.

Jackson: Would that be appropriate?

Seunim: Of course, focusing your mind comes before maintaining position.

쉬어가는 코너

Punna, grow full with good qualities
Like the moon on the fifteenth day.
With discernment at total fullness,
Burst the mass of darkness.

– *Therigatha*

뿐나여, 보름달이 둥글게 차오르듯
선한 성품을 닦아 키워라.
바른 지혜가 차오를 때 그것으로
무지의 어둠을 깨뜨려라.

– 장로니게

Chapter 2

Exploring the Temple
사찰 안내

Unit 1

Daejeokgwang-jeon (The Vairocara Hall)

Seunim: This is called Daejeokgwang-jeon, or the Vairocara Hall. This is Girim-sa Temple's main Dharma hall.

Martin: Which Buddha is enshrined here?

Seunim: The main Buddha in the center is Vairocana Buddha.

Martin: He has a unique hand posture.

Seunim: Yes, a Buddha's hand posture is called a "*su-in*" or "mudra." This particular mudra is called "*jigweonin*." Four fingers of Buddha's right hand are holding his left index finger.

Martin: Is there a special meaning behind it?

Seunim: It means the land of Buddha and the mundane world are not two but one.

▶▶ 대적광전

스님: 이곳은 대적광전입니다. 기림사에서 가장 중심이 되는 법당이지요.
마틴: 그럼 어떤 부처님을 모셨나요?
스님: 가운데 모신 주불은 비로자나불입니다.
마틴: 손 모양이 특이하군요.
스님: 예, 이 수인은 '지권인'이라 하는데 왼손의 집게손가락을 펴서 오른손으로 감싸는 모양을 하고 있어요.
마틴: 여기에 어떤 의미가 담겨있나요?
스님: 부처님의 세계와 인간 세계의 진리가 둘이 아니고 하나라는 뜻입니다.

Words & Phrases

❖ **Which~** 어떠한
- Which Buddha is painted in this picture? (어떠한 부처님이 그려진 그림인가요?)
- Which color do you like best? (어떠한 색깔을 좋아하세요?)
- Which path should we take on this hike? (어떤 길로 산행을 해 볼까요?)

❖ *mudra* 수인
- *Mudra* means a Buddha's hand posture. (수인은 부처의 손 모양입니다.)
- Are there many different kinds of *mudras*? (수인에는 여러 종류가 있나요?)

❖ **finger** 손가락
- thumb (엄지), index finger (검지), middle finger (중지), ring finger (약지), little finger (새끼 손가락)

Pair Work
Practice by substituting the underlined words with other proper words and phrases.

Seunim: This is <u>what we call</u> Daejeokgwang-jeon, or the Vairocara Hall. This is <u>known as</u> Girim-sa Temple's main Dharma hall.

Martin: <u>What is the name of the Buddha who is enshrined here?</u>

Seunim: The main Buddha in the center <u>is called</u> Vairocana Buddha.

Martin: <u>What can you tell me about Vairocana Buddha?</u>

Seunim: <u>Vairocana means "The Luminous One," and is often known as the Buddha of Great Light.</u>

Martin: His hand posture is <u>very unique.</u>

Seunim: Yes, a Buddha's hand posture is called a "*su-in*" or "*mudra*." This particular one is called "*jigweonin*" where four fingers of Buddha's right hand are wrapped around his left index finger.

Unit 2 — Gwaneum-jeon (The Avalokitesvara Hall)

Seunim: This is Gwaneum-jeon where Avalokitesvara is enshrined.

Anna: Avalokitesvara is the Bodhisattva of Great Compassion, right?

Seunim: Great answer! Many Koreans love and respect Avalokitesvara.

Anna: I think Western Buddhists feel the same way.

Seunim: Yes, the Bodhisattva of Great Compassion listens to all sentient beings in the world.

Anna: Seunim, is Avalokitesvara male or female?

Seunim: In some Buddhist paintings in Asia, Avalokitesvara is depicted as female, but originally, this bodhisattva transcends gender.

觀音殿 관음전

스님: 이곳은 관음전입니다. 관세음보살을 모신 법당이지요.

애나: 관세음보살은 자비의 보살이지요?

스님: 그렇습니다. 많은 한국인들이 관세음보살을 좋아하지요.

애나: 저희 서양 불자들도 좋아합니다.

스님: 예, 중생의 모든 소리를 다 들어주신다는 보살님이니까요.

애나: 스님, 그런데 관세음보살은 여자인가요, 남자인가요?

스님: 동양의 일부 불화에서는 여성으로 묘사되기도 하지만 본래는 성별을 초월합니다.

Words & Phrases

❖ **~right?** 그렇지요?
- Nice weather, right? (오늘은 날씨가 참 좋지요?)
- You are Kevin, right? (당신이 케빈이지요?)
- You will arrive next Wednesday, right? (다음 주 수요일 도착이시지요?)

❖ **feel the same way (as) / agree with / concur with** 동감하다
- We all felt the same way about Korea's wonderful culture.
  (우리 모두 한국 문화의 우수함에 동감했습니다.)
- I feel very much the same way as Sarah. (사라의 의견에 깊이 동감합니다.)
- I believe he agreed with my thoughts. (그도 저의 생각에 동감했을 겁니다.)

❖ **or** 아니면, 또는, 혹은
- Are you tired or feeling energetic? (피곤한가요 아니면 힘이 넘치나요?)
- Today shall we meditate first or afterwards? (오늘은 명상을 먼저 할까요 아니면 나중에 할까요?)
- Does anyone have a question or something they would like to share?
  (궁금하거나 또는 나누고 싶은 의견이 있으신가요?)

❖ **transcends / surpass / go beyond** 초월하다
- Their friendship surpasses their age difference. (그들의 우정은 나이 차이를 초월한 우정입니다.)
- The result is beyond everyone's expectations. (우리 모두의 기대 이상의 결과입니다.)

Pair Work
Practice by substituting the underlined words with other proper words and phrases.

Seunim: This is Gwaneum-jeon and <u>it enshrines</u> Avalokitesvara.

Anna: Avalokitesvara is <u>known as the</u> Bodhisattva of Great Compassion, <u>correct?</u>

Seunim: Outstanding! Many Koreans <u>cherish</u> Avalokitesvara.

Anna: I think Western Buddhists <u>would agree as well.</u>

Seunim: Yes, the Bodhisattva of Great Compassion <u>looks after</u> all sentient beings in the world.

Anna: Seunim, <u>the statue of Avalokitesvara here has a womanly figure.</u>

Seunim: In some Asian Buddhist art, Avalokitesvara is illustrated as a female, but originally, that bodhisattva surpasses gender.

Unit 3

Mita-jeon (The Amitabha Hall)

Seunim: This is the hall where Amitabha Buddha is enshrined.

Martin: Which Buddha is Amitabha Buddha?

Seunim: Amitabha Buddha is the Buddha who resides in the Pure Land of utmost bliss, which is commonly referred to as the "Western Paradise."

Martin: In Christianity, there is Heaven. In Buddhism, there is Pure Land.

Seunim: Yes, when a person dies, we pray to Amitabha Buddha that he or she be reborn in the Pure Land.

Martin: Does such a place really exist somewhere in the west?

Seunim: Well, in Buddhism, everything starts from one's mind. Therefore, if one's mind is happy, he's already in the Pure Land. If one is not happy, wouldn't he be in hell?

▶▶ 미타전

스님: 이곳은 아미타불을 모신 법당입니다.
마틴: 아미타불은 어떤 부처님이신가요?
스님: 우리가 흔히 '극락'이라고 부르는 정토에 계시는 부처님입니다.
마틴: 기독교에는 천당이 있는데 불교에도 극락이 있군요.
스님: 예, 그래서 사람이 죽으면 아미타불께 기도를 드리며 부디 극락에서 태어나게 해달라고 기도를 합니다.
마틴: 그런 곳이 정말 서쪽에 있나요?
스님: 글쎄요, 불교에서는 모든 것이 '마음'으로부터 출발하지요. 그러니까 이 마음이 행복하면 극락이고 이 마음이 불행하면 지옥이 아닐까요?

Words & Phrases

❖ **commonly referred to as / commonly known as** 흔히 알고 있는
  - *Gimchi* is commonly known as Korea's signature dish.
    (김치는 한국을 대표하는 음식으로 알려져 있습니다.)

❖ **the Pure Land** 정토 / **the Pure Land Sect** 정토종

❖ **Christian** (형용사) / **Christianity** (명사) 크리스찬
  (Cf. 개신교, 가톨릭 등 모든 기독교 종파에 대한 총칭)
  - That Christian church is very beautiful. (저 교회는 매우 아름답네요.)
  - Christianity has a long history. (그리스도교는 긴 역사를 가지고 있습니다.)

❖ **Catholic** 가톨릭 (형용사, 명사로 가톨릭 신자) / **Catholicism** (명사) 가톨릭 종교 / **Protestant** 개신교 신자 / **Protestantism** 개신교
  - Jenny is a Catholic. (제니는 가톨릭 신자입니다.)
  - Jenny believes in Catholicism. (제니는 가톨릭 종교를 믿습니다.)

❖ **somewhere** ~어디엔가
  - Somewhere in this book, there is a recipe for monastic temple cuisine.
    (이 책 안에 사찰 음식 조리법이 들어 있습니다.)
  - Somewhere over the roof, I can hear the birds chirping.
    (지붕 너머 어디에선가 새들이 지저귀는 소리가 들립니다.)
  - Somewhere in the first-aid kit, we have a bandage. (구급상자 어디엔가 붕대가 있습니다.)

Pair Work
Practice by substituting the underlined words with other proper words and phrases.

Seunim: This is the hall with Amitabha Buddha.

Martin: Who is Amitabha Buddha?

Seunim: Amitabha Buddha is the Buddha who lives in the Pure Land of utmost bliss, which is commonly referred to as the "Western Paradise."

Martin: Do you believe such a place truly exists?

Seunim: Well, in Buddhism, everything originates from one's mind. We believe the Pure Land is already with us here and now. We just do not see it yet.

Unit 4

Jijang-jeon (The Ksitigarbha Hall)

Seunim: This is the Jijang-jeon where Ksitigarbha Bodhisattva is enshrined.

Anna: This bodhisattva's head is different from the others.

Seunim: Good point! Unlike others, his head is shaved like a seunim, and he is wearing a hood.

Anna: Perhaps that is why he feels very familiar.

Seunim: Ksitigarbha Bodhisattva has made a great vow.

Anna: What would that be?

Seunim: He vowed not to become a Buddha until he saves all beings in hell.

Anna: Wow! That is indeed a great vow!

지장전

스님: 이곳은 지장보살을 모신 지장전입니다.

애나: 보살님 머리가 좀 특이한데요.

스님: 예, 다른 보살들과 달리 스님처럼 삭발을 하고 머리에 두건을 썼습니다.

애나: 그래서 그런지 스님처럼 친근하게 느껴집니다.

스님: 지장보살은 커다란 서원을 실천하고 있습니다.

애나: 그게 무엇인가요?

스님: 지옥의 중생들을 다 구제할 때까지 성불하지 않겠다고 했어요.

애나: 와, 정말 큰 서원이군요.

Words & Phrases

❖ **different from** ~와는 다르다
- The design of this stupa is different from the others. (이 탑의 디자인은 다른 것들과 다릅니다.)
- The directions from the GPS are different from those of the tourist office.
  (내비게이션에 나오는 길 안내는 관광 안내소에서 준 것과 다릅니다.)
- What we are learning today is different than yesterday. (오늘 배울 내용은 어제와 다릅니다.)

❖ **like + (명사)** ~처럼
- The territory of Korea looks like a tiger. (대한민국 영토는 호랑이처럼 생겼습니다.)
- It looks like it's going to rain. (오늘은 비가 올 것처럼 보입니다.)
- Seunim laughed like an innocent child. (스님이 순박한 아이처럼 웃으셨습니다.)

❖ **vow** 다짐하다 / **make a vow** 서원을 세우다
- Sarah vowed to dedicate her life to children all over the world.
  (사라는 앞으로 세상의 어린이들을 위해 살겠다고 다짐했다.)
- Jeffery and Jessica vowed to marry. (제프리와 제시카는 부부가 되기로 서약했다.)
- A person who becomes ordained vows to dedicate his or her life to save all sentient beings.
  (출가자는 일체중생을 구원하겠다는 서원을 지니는 사람이다.)

❖ **indeed / really / absolutely** 정말, 확실히
- Yes, indeed. (네, 정말 그래요.)
- You are indeed a devout Buddhist. (당신은 정말 독실한 불자시군요.)

Pair Work

Practice by substituting the underlined words with other proper words and phrases.

Seunim: Jijang-jeon is the shrine for Ksitigarbha Bodhisattva.

Anna: He looks different from other bodhisattvas.

Seunim: Good point! Unlike others, his head is shaved like a seunim, and he has a hood on his head.

Anna: That's it! I thought that he looks rather like a seunim.

Seunim: Ksitigarbha Bodhisattva is well known for his great vow.

Anna: What is his vow?

Seunim: He has vowed to become a Buddha only after he saves all beings in hell.

Anna: That sure is a great vow!

Unit 5: Josa-jeon (The Hall of Patriarchs)

Seunim: This is the shrine of patriarchs.

Martin: Does that mean the hall enshrines patriarchs?

Seunim: Yes, and the founder of the temple and other esteemed masters are enshrined here as well.

Martin: Whose portrait is that in the center?

Seunim: That is the portrait of Venerable Na-ong. To his left, we have great Venerable Jigong, and to his right, we have Master Muhak.

≫ 조사전

스님: 이곳은 조사전입니다.

마틴: 조사전에는 조사들을 모시나요?

스님: 예, 조사들 뿐 아니라 절의 창건주, 고승들도 모십니다.

마틴: 저기 중앙에 계신 진영은 누구를 그린 것이지요?

스님: 이곳 신륵사 조사전의 경우 불단 중앙에는 나옹스님을, 그 좌우에는 지공스님과 무학대사의 진영을 모시고 있습니다.

Words & Phrases

❖ **Does that mean ~ ?** ～한 뜻인가요? ～인가요?
- Does that mean children can participate? (아이들도 참여할 수 있다는 뜻인가요?)
- Does that mean temples are open to everyone? (사찰은 모두에게 열려 있나요?)
- Does that mean *naengmyeon* is only for the summer? (냉면은 여름에만 먹는 음식인가요?)

❖ **~ as well / not only ~ but also ~** ～뿐만 아니라, 물론
- This temple boasts a long history and a unique tradition.
  (이 사찰은 오랜 역사와 전통도 자랑하는 곳입니다.)
- A Templestay program provides a chance to enjoy Korea's traditional culture as well as to take a look at oneself. (템플스테이는 한국의 전통문화 체험은 물론 자기 자신을 돌아보는 기회입니다.)

❖ **boast / be proud of / prides oneself on** 자랑하다
- Koreans are very proud of their Buddhist heritage.
  (한국인들은 자신들의 불교 유산에 대해 아주 자랑스러워 합니다.)
- You can rightly take pride in the worldwide recognition of Hangeul.
  (한글의 우수성에 대해서는 가히 자랑할 만하다.)

❖ **whose** 누구의
- Whose shoes are these? (이 신발은 누구의 것인가요?)
- Whose *baru* bowls are these? (이 발우는 누구의 것인가요?)
- Whose watch is this? (이 시계는 누구의 것인가요?)
- Whose turn is it to read the book? (책을 읽을 차례는 누구인가요?)

Pair Work
Practice by substituting the underlined words with other proper words and phrases.

Seunim: This shrine is dedicated to the patriarchs.
Martin: Is the hall dedicated only to the patriarchs?
Seunim: No, the temple also honors the temple's founder and other esteemed masters as well.
Martin: Who is it in the portrait over there?
Seunim: That portrait is of Venerable Na-ong.

Chapter 3

Phone Conversations
전화 대화

Unit 1

Inquiring about the Templestay Program

Seunim: This is Jikji-sa Temple. How may I help you?

Martin: When I go to a weekend Templestay, do I have to attend all of the programs?

Seunim: You do not have to. We do recommend you to attend and experience as much as you can, but it is not mandatory.

Martin: I am a Catholic, so I don't feel comfortable attending the Dharma service.

Seunim: I am glad you mentioned that. A Templestay is mostly a cultural experience, rather than a religious event.

Martin: I still don't feel comfortable. However, I really would like to experience what monastic life is like.

Seunim: I understand. During the Dharma service, you are welcome to sit at the back, or if you wish, you do not have to attend the service at all.

▶▶ 템플스테이 프로그램 문의

스님: 직지사입니다. 무엇을 도와드릴까요?

마틴: 주말 템플스테이를 하려면 모든 프로그램에 다 참여해야 합니까?

스님: 꼭 그렇지는 않습니다.
물론 모든 프로그램에 고루 참여하시라고 저희가 권해 드리긴 하지만 의무 사항은 아닙니다.

마틴: 저는 가톨릭 신자라서 예불을 하는 것이 꺼려집니다.

스님: 템플스테이는 문화 체험을 목적으로 한 것입니다. 종교 행사는 아니지요.

마틴: 그래도 왠지 내키지가 않아요. 하지만 사찰 생활은 꼭 체험해보고 싶습니다.

스님: 그렇다면 예불 시간에 법당 뒤쪽에 조용히 앉아계세요. 영 내키지 않으신다면 참석하지 않아도 됩니다.

Words & Phrases

❖ **have to + (동사)** 반드시 해야 하다
- You have to bring medicine for your medical condition. (자신에게 필요한 약은 꼭 가져와야 합니다.)
- You have to bring your own ID. (신분증은 반드시 가져와야 합니다.)

❖ **don't have to + (동사)** 반드시 하지 않아도 된다
- You don't have to write down your address. (주소는 기재하지 않아도 됩니다..)
- You don't have to join us for hiking. (우리와 산행에 동행하지 않아도 됩니다.)

❖ **mandatory** 의무적인
- It is mandatory for Korean men to do the military service. (한국 남자는 병역 의무를 가진다.)
- It is mandatory for monks to get permission before entering into a retreat.
  (스님은 안거를 들어가기 전에 허락을 받아야 한다.)

❖ **feel uncomfortable / feel reluctant to** 내키지 않다, 꺼리다
- He seems a little reluctant to prostrate himself. (절하는 것을 조금 꺼려하는 것처럼 보였다.)
- People are reluctant to change. (사람들은 변화하는 것을 꺼린다.)

❖ **be welcome to~ / feel free to~** 을 마음대로 해도 된다, 자유롭게 ~하라
- You are welcome to stay longer. (더 머무셔도 됩니다.)
- Feel free to eat as much as you like. (마음껏 드셔도 됩니다.)
- You are welcome to go in and take a look. (들어가서 구경하셔도 됩니다.)

❖ **do + (동사)** : 강조용법
- I do recommend it. (꼭 추천합니다.)
- I do like swimming. (저 수영 매우 좋아해요.)

❖ **what~ is like** ~가 어떠한지
- I wonder what monastic life is like. (사찰 생활이 어떤지 궁금합니다.)
- Can you imagine what religion will be like in 100 years?
  (100년 후에 종교가 어떻게 될지 상상이 가니?)

Pair Work — Practice by substituting the underlined words with other proper words and phrases.

Seunim: You've reached Jikji-sa Temple. May I help you?

Martin: When I attend the weekend Templestay, must I participate in all programs? I'm a Catholic and therefore reluctant to attend the Dharma service.

Seunim: I'm glad you mentioned that. Mostly, a Templestay is a cultural experience. You don't have to attend any program that you think is against your religious beliefs.

Martin: Although I still don't feel comfortable, I'd really like to experience what monastic life is like.

Seunim: I understand. During the Dharma service, feel free to sit at the back, or, if you wish, you are not required to attend the service at all.

Unit 2 Inquiring about the Temple Facility

Seunim: Hello, this is Jikji-sa Temple. How can I assist you?
Anna: How many people are assigned to a room during the Templestay?
Seunim: About three to four people will sleep in a room.
Anna: Is the bathroom located outside?
Seunim: No, there is a modern bathroom inside each room.
Anna: Wow! So is the dormitory a modern style building?
Seunim: No, it is a traditional Korean style architecture built with wood, clay and paper, and it was built only with environmentally friendly materials.
Anna: Sounds amazing. I am looking forward to it!

▶▶ 템플스테이 시설 문의

스님: 직지사입니다. 무엇을 도와 드릴까요?
애나: 템플스테이에 참여하면 몇 사람이 한 방에서 자나요?
스님: 3~4명이 한방에서 잡니다.
애나: 화장실은 방 밖에 있나요?
스님: 아닙니다. 방마다 현대식 욕실이 딸려 있습니다.
애나: 와, 그럼 현대식 건물인가요?
스님: 아니요. 전통 한옥 건물입니다. 자재로 쓰인 목재, 황토, 종이 등도 모두 친환경 소재입니다.
애나: 와, 멋지네요. 기대가 됩니다.

Words & Phrases

❖ **How can I + (동사) you?** 어떻게 ~해 드릴까요?
  - How can I assist you? (어떻게 도와 드릴까요?)
  - How can I support you? (어떻게 힘이 되어 드릴까요?)

❖ **be located** 위치해 있다
  - Jikji-sa Temple is located on Mt. Hwangaksan. (직지사는 황악산 안에 위치하고 있습니다.)
  - The library is located next to the bank. (도서관은 은행 옆에 위치해 있다.)

❖ **each + (명사)** ~마다
  - There is a shower facility in each room. (모든 방마다 샤워 시설이 있습니다.)
  - Each temple has an abbot, who is the head seunim. (각각의 사찰마다 주지 스님이 계십니다.)
  - Each participant will receive a certificate of participation.
    (참여자마다 프로그램 수료증을 드립니다.)
  - In each corner of the temple, you can see the hard work of seunims.
    (사찰 구석구석마다 스님들의 땀이 배어 있습니다.)

❖ **~friendly** 친화적인, 적합한
  - environmentally friendly / earth-friendly / eco-friendly (친환경적인)
  - user-friendly (사용하기 쉬운)
  - child-friendly environment (아이들에게 적합한 환경)

Pair Work
Practice by substituting the underlined words with other proper words and phrases.

Seunim: Hello, this is Jikji-sa Temple. <u>May</u> I assist you?

Anna: How many people <u>do you assign</u> to a room during a Templestay?

Seunim: About three to four people.

Anna: <u>Is the bathroom outside?</u>

Seunim: No, <u>inside each room</u> is a modern bathroom.

Anna: <u>How about showers?</u>

Seunim: <u>All bathrooms are equipped with showers.</u>

Anna: Sounds <u>fantastic. I cannot wait!</u>

Unit 3 — Inquiring about Meals during a Templestay Program

Seunim: Thank you for calling Jikji-sa Temple. How may I help you?

Martin: Hello, I would like to know what kind of food you serve during the two-day Templestay.

Seunim: We serve healthy Korean meals.

Martin: Does it include meat and fish?

Seunim: No, all meals are vegetarian.

Martin: Will I eat at a table?

Seunim: For dinners, yes. But for breakfast, we all sit on the floor and eat a traditional *baru gongyang* meal.

템플스테이 식사 문의

스님: 직지사입니다. 무엇을 도와 드릴까요?

마틴: 예, 템플스테이에선 이틀 동안 어떤 음식을 먹나요?

스님: 몸에 좋은 한식을 먹습니다.

마틴: 그럼 고기와 생선도 주나요?

스님: 아니요, 모든 식사는 채식입니다.

마틴: 식사는 서양식 식탁에서 하나요?

스님: 예, 저녁 식사는 그렇게 합니다. 하지만 아침 식사는 바닥에 앉아 발우공양으로 먹습니다.

Words & Phrases

❖ **I would like to + (동사) / I want to + (동사)** ~하고 싶습니다
- I would like to get more information on your program.
  (프로그램 내용을 더욱 자세히 알고 싶습니다.)
- I would like to find out more about Buddhism. (불교에 대해 더 알고 싶습니다.)
- I would like to explore the history of Hwaeom-sa. (화엄사의 역사에 대해 알고 싶습니다.)

❖ **serve** 제공하다, 섬기다
- All meals served are from a vegan-friendly menu. (제공되는 식사는 비건에 친화적인 식단입니다.)
- Meals are served at designated times only. (식사는 정해진 시간에만 제공됩니다.)
- He served his teacher all his life. (그는 평생 동안 스승님을 섬겼다.)

Pair Work
Practice by substituting the underlined words with other proper words and phrases.

Seunim: Thank you for calling Jikji-sa Temple. May I help you?

Martin: Hello, I'd like to know what you serve to eat during the two-day Templestay.

Seunim: We serve healthy Korean meals.

Martin: It is made with meat and fish?

Seunim: No, the temple meals are vegetarian.

Martin: How do we eat?

Seunim: For breakfast, we eat a traditional *baru gongyang* meal sitting on the floor; for dinner, we dine at a table.

Unit 4

Bedtime at a Templestay Program

Seunim: Hello, this is Jikji-sa Temple. How may I help you?
Anna: Hello, what time should participants go to bed during a Templestay?
Seunim: At 9 p.m.
Anna: Wow! That's very early! I am a night owl, so I am not sure if I will be able to fall asleep.
Seunim: I am sure you will have no problem. You will be very tired after your long trip, and you will go straight into our program after registration at 2:30 p.m.
Anna: I hope so.
Seunim: Also, our day starts at 3 a.m., which means you should get plenty of sleep beforehand.
Anna: Oh my goodness, that is very early!

》 템플스테이 취침 시간

스님: 직지사입니다. 무엇을 도와 드릴까요?
애나: 템플스테이 참가자의 취침 시간은 몇 시인가요?
스님: 오후 9시입니다.
애나: 와, 그렇게나 일찍요? 저는 본래 늦게 자는 사람이라서 잠이 올지 모르겠네요.
스님: 아마 잘 올 겁니다. 그날 장거리 여행을 해서 피곤하실 뿐 아니라, 오후 2시 30분 등록 이후 계속 프로그램에 참여하실 테니까요.
애나: 저도 그러길 바랍니다.
스님: 다음 날 새벽 3시에 기상하셔야 하니까 더더욱 일찍 주무셔야지요.
애나: 맙소사! 그렇게 일찍요!

Words & Phrases

❖ **What time should I + (동사)?** 몇 시에 ~해야 하나요?
  - What time should I wake up? (몇 시에 기상해야 하나요?)
  - What time should I come back? (몇 시까지 돌아와야 하나요?)

❖ **(명사/대명사) + should + (동사) + by (시간)** 몇 시까지 ~해야 합니다
  - You should turn your lights off by 9 p.m. (오후 9시까지 소등해야 합니다.)
  - You should report to the Dharma Hall by 10 a.m. (대법당에 오전 10시까지 와야 합니다.)
  - We should return to the temple by 4 p.m. (우리는 사찰에 오후 4시까지 돌아가야 합니다.)
  - The students should leave by 3 p.m. to catch their bus.
    (학생들은 버스를 타기 위해 오후 3시에는 떠나야 합니다.)

❖ **Wow, (명사/대명사) + is / are+ very + (형용사)!** (감탄사)와! 정말 + (형용사)!
  - Wow, that's very beautiful! (와! 정말 아름답네요!)
  - Wow, you are very knowledgeable! (와! 정말 지식이 깊으시네요!)
  - Wow, the scenery is spectacular! (와, 경치가 웅장하네요!)

❖ **I am sure (that) / certain (that)** 그럴 겁니다
  - I am sure (that) your family misses you. (아마 가족이 당신을 매우 보고 싶어할 겁니다.)
  - I am certain (that) the temple food helps seunims with their practice.
    (아마 사찰 음식은 스님의 수행에 많은 도움이 될 겁니다.)
  - I am positive (that) your hard work today will pay off soon. (아마 오늘의 노력이 곧 빛을 발할 겁니다.)

Pair Work

Practice by substituting the underlined words with other proper words and phrases.

Seunim: Hello, this is Jikji-sa Temple. How may I assist you?

Anna: Hello, what time do participants retire to bed during a Templestay?

Seunim: At 9 p.m.

Anna: Wow, how early! I'm a night owl, so I'm uncertain if I can fall asleep at 9 p.m.

Seunim: I'm sure you won't have a problem. You'll be very tired after your long trip and will go straight into our program after registration at 2:30 p.m.

Anna: I hope so.

Seunim: Lastly, our day starts at 3 a.m., meaning you should rest plenty beforehand.

Anna: Unbelievable! That's really early!

Unit 5

Suggesting a Templestay to a Friend

Anna: Hi Martin, this is Anna!

Martin: Hi Anna, it's been a while! How have you been?

Anna: I am doing well. How about yourself?

Martin: I am doing great. What's going on?

Anna: Well, I participated in a Templestay at Jikji-sa Temple last weekend. I really enjoyed it, and I thought you'd like it too.

Martin: Oh, I see. I went to a Templestay at Beomeo-sa Temple a while ago. I had a great time.

Anna: That's good to hear. When I went to the mountains, my mind just became very peaceful.

Martin: Yes, when I got up early with the Buddhist monks and practiced with them, I also felt my mind becoming very calm and peaceful.

▶▶ 템플스테이 권유

애나: 여보세요, 마틴! 나 애나예요.

마틴: 애나, 오랜만입니다. 잘 지냈어요?

애나: 네, 마틴도요?

마틴: 그럼요. 그런데 웬일로 전화를 주셨나요?

애나: 제가 지난 주말에 직지사 템플스테이에 다녀왔는데요, 너무 좋아서 마틴도 가보라고 전화했어요.

마틴: 저도 얼마 전 범어사 템플스테이에 다녀왔는데 참 좋더군요.

애나: 그랬군요. 산에 가니까 마음이 저절로 평화로워졌어요.

마틴: 예, 그리고 스님들처럼 일찍 일어나서 수행하니까 마음이 고요하고 편안해지더군요.

Words & Phrases

❖ 안부인사 – 질문
  - How is life treating you? (요즘 어떻게 지내시나요?)
  - What's going on? (잘 지내나요?)

❖ 안부인사 – 답변
  - I am doing fine. (잘 지냅니다.)
  - Everything's well. (만사형통 합니다.)

❖ **I really enjoyed +** (명사/동명사) 정말 즐거웠습니다
  - I really enjoyed the summer camp. (여름 캠프는 정말 즐거웠습니다.)
  - I very much enjoyed my Templestay. (템플스테이는 정말 좋았습니다.)
  - Everyone enjoyed their *baru gongyang* experience. (우리 모두 발우공양 참여를 뜻깊어 했습니다.)
  - I really enjoyed reading that book. (그 책을 읽는 것이 정말 즐거웠어요.)

Pair Work
Practice by substituting the underlined words with other proper words and phrases.

Anna: Hi Martin, Anna here!

Martin: Hi Anna, it's been a while! How are you doing?

Anna: I am doing well. How about yourself?

Martin: I'm doing great. What's going on?

Anna: Well, I went to a Templestay at Jikji-sa last weekend and really enjoyed it. I thought you'd like it too.

Martin: Oh, nice. I went to one at Beomeo-sa a while ago and had a great time.

Anna: That's good to hear! Going to the mountains, I experienced peace.

Martin: Yes, getting up early and practicing with the Buddhist monks, I also felt very calm and peaceful.

쉬어가는 코너

As a deer in the wilds, unfettered,
Goes wherever it wants,
A wise person, valuing freedom,
Wanders alone as a rhinoceros horn.

– *Sutta Nipata*

고삐에 매이지 않은 야생 사슴이
어디든 원하는 곳으로 가듯이
자유를 소중히 여기는 현자는
무소의 뿔처럼 혼자서 간다.

– 숫타니파타

Chapter 4

The Temple Life
사찰 생활

Unit 1

Importance of Being Punctual

Seunim: Martin, please remember that when you are at a temple, being punctual is very important.

Martin: What do you mean?

Seunim: You should keep to the schedule for going to bed, getting up in the morning and eating meals.

Martin: I believe you are saying that I should do things together with the others, being mindful of others in eating, sleeping and getting up.

Seunim: You are correct. If you stay up late and keep the lights on, then others will be disturbed.

Martin: Yes, I had a similar experience in the past, so I understand.

Seunim: There's one more thing. In the temple community, we follow the rule of eating only during the official mealtime. Therefore, please be punctual at mealtimes as well.

▶▶ 시간 지키기

스님: 마틴, 절에서 생활하시는 동안에는 정해진 시간을 엄수해야 합니다.

마틴: 어떤 시간을 말씀하시는지요?

스님: 취침, 기상, 공양 시간을 말합니다.

마틴: 네, 함께 자고, 함께 일어나고, 함께 식사하라는 말씀이군요.

스님: 예, 마틴이 늦게까지 잠을 안 자고 불을 켜고 있으면 함께 자는 사람이 잠을 잘 못자겠지요.

마틴: 네, 저도 그런 경험이 있으니 이해합니다.

스님: 또 불가에서는 '때 아닌 때 먹어서는 안 된다'는 규정이 있습니다. 그러니 공양 시간도 꼭 지켜주세요.

Words & Phrases

❖ **a team player** 단체 활동을 잘 하는 사람
- Freddy was voted a team player because he helped other participants.
(프레디는 다른 참여자들을 잘 도와주어 팀 플레이어로 뽑혔습니다.)

❖ **keep to ~ / obey / observe / follow** (약속, 합의 등을) 지키다
- They decided to keep to the previous agreement. (그들은 이전 합의를 지키기로 결정했다.)
- You must keep to the rules even if you think they're unfair.
(불공정하게 보이더라도 규칙은 지켜야 한다.)

❖ **If + (현재형 동사) + then + (미래형 동사)** 하면 ~된다
- If you come well prepared, then you will be pleased. (준비를 잘 하고 오면 마음이 편안할 거예요.)
- If you go to bed late, then you will be very tired the next day.
(늦게까지 자지 않으면 다음 날 매우 피곤한 거예요.)
- If you follow the instructions, then you will learn to meditate.
(설명을 잘 따라 하면 명상하는 법을 배울 수 있습니다.)

❖ **punctual / on time** 시간을 준수하다
- Please be punctual for tomorrow's Dharma service. (내일 법회 시간을 준수해 주세요.)
- He is famous for his punctuality. (그는 시간을 잘 지키기로 유명합니다.)

Pair Work
Practice by substituting the underlined words with other proper words and phrases.

Seunim: Martin, please remember: when you're at a temple, punctuality is very important.

Martin: What do you mean?

Seunim: You should obey the times for retiring to bed, awaking in the morning, and partaking in meals.

Martin: So I should be a team player and sleep, awaken and enjoy meals with others.

Seunim: Correct. If you stay up late and keep the lights on, you will disturb others.

Martin: Yes, having had a similar experience in the past, I understand.

Seunim: There's one more thing. In the Buddhist community, we strictly eat only during the official mealtimes. Therefore, please be punctual for mealtimes, too.

Unit 2 — Meal Etiquette

Seunim: At the temple, one may not leave any leftovers behind when you eat.

Anna: That was a challenge for me.

Seunim: It's not very difficult. Just take what you can eat at one time.

Anna: "Taking what I can eat" is the difficult part. When I am hungry, I always take more!

Seunim: Of course. That is why this is a great way of learning to control one's desire.

Anna: I often heard the phrase, "In Buddhist temples, not even a single grain of rice gets wasted."

Seunim: Yes, that reminds us to be aware and thankful for our patrons' gracious donations.

공양 예절

스님: 공양할 때는 절대로 음식을 남겨서는 안 됩니다.
애나: 제 경험으로는 그게 좀 어려웠어요.
스님: 자기가 먹을 만큼만 덜어 먹으면 어렵지 않아요.
애나: '자기가 먹을 만큼만'이 어려워요. 배가 고플 때는 음식을 많이 가져오게 되거든요.
스님: 물론 그렇지요. 그러니 욕망을 절제하는 법을 배우는 것도 됩니다.
애나: '절에서는 쌀 한 톨도 함부로 버리지 않는다'는 이야기를 자주 들었어요.
스님: 예, 그만큼 시주의 은혜를 소중히 여기고 감사한 마음을 가지라는 말씀이지요.

Words & Phrases

❖ **may not + (동사)** 하면 안 됩니다
- Seunims may not get married. (스님은 결혼을 할 수 없습니다.)
- One may not walk on the lawn. (잔디밭에 들어가면 안 됩니다.)
- One may not eat before others. (먼저 먹어서는 안 됩니다.)

❖ **may + (동사)** 해도 됩니다
- You may share your challenges. (어려운 점을 말해보세요.)
- You may ask questions. (질문을 해도 됩니다.)

❖ **a great way to + (동사)** 좋은 방법입니다
- Reading sutras is a great way to understand Buddhism.
  (경전을 읽는 것은 불교를 이해하기에 좋은 방법입니다.)
- Drinking tea is a great way to help one's practice. (차를 마시는 것은 수행을 하는 좋은 방법입니다.)

❖ **remind ~ to do ~** 를 해야 한다는 것을 상기시켜 줍니다
- Please remind me to stop by the post office. (내가 우체국에 들러야 한다는 것을 상기시켜 주세요.)
- How do I remind my professor to write a letter of recommendation?
  (교수님이 저에게 그 추천장을 써주셔야 한다는 것을 어떻게 상기시켜 드리죠?)

Pair Work
Practice by substituting the underlined words with other proper words and phrases.

Seunim: In the temple, please do not leave any leftovers.

Anna: That was very hard for me to follow.

Seunim: It's not that hard. Just choose as much as you can eat.

Anna: Grabbing as much as I think I can eat is very hard. When I am hungry, I automatically take more!

Seunim: Of course. That is why this is a wonderful way of learning to tame one's desire.

Anna: I have heard the phrase, "In Buddhist temples, not even a single grain of rice gets wasted."

Seunim: Yes, that guides us to be aware and thankful for our patrons' gracious donations.

Unit 3

Shoe Etiquette

Seunim: Martin, please make sure not to drag your feet when walking.

Martin: Oh, I am very sorry. I was in a hurry, so I didn't put my shoes on properly.

Seunim: In the temple, every action you take through speaking, thinking and moving is a part of practice.

Martin: I get it. I should be mindful even when I take my shoes off.

Seunim: That's a great idea! Make sure that your shoes are not carelessly tossed aside before you enter a building.

Martin: Yes, I will place them neatly outside the door before I enter.

▶▶ 신발 관리

스님: 마틴, 신발을 끌고 다니면 안 됩니다.

마틴: 앗, 죄송합니다. 마음이 급해서 미처 제대로 못 신었어요.

스님: 사찰에서는 일상생활에서 하는 말하고 생각하고 움직이는 모든 것이 다 수행입니다.

마틴: 그렇군요. 신발을 벗을 때도 마음을 챙기면서 벗어야겠어요.

스님: 좋은 생각입니다. 신발을 아무렇게나 벗어놓고 그냥 가면 안 되겠지요.

마틴: 네, 벗은 다음에 손으로 가지런히 정리해 놓고 들어가겠습니다.

Words & Phrases

❖ **Please make sure to~** 주의해 주세요, 꼭 ~해 주세요
- Please make sure to pay respect to seunims. (스님께는 예의를 갖춰 주세요.)
- Please make sure to wear comfortable shoes tomorrow. (내일은 꼭 편한 신발을 신어 주세요.)
- Please make sure to wear sunscreen lotion when we go hiking.
  (산행 시에는 반드시 썬블락(자외선 차단제)을 발라 주세요.)

❖ **a part of ~** ~의 일부
- Temple cuisine is an important part of Korean Buddhist culture.
  (사찰 음식은 한국 불교문화의 중요한 일부입니다.)
- Resting your mind is an essential part of the Templestay program.
  (마음을 쉬는 것은 템플스테이의 중요한 목표 중 하나입니다.)

❖ **neatly / orderly / in order** 꼼꼼하게, 깔끔하게
- His room was neatly organized. (그의 방은 꼼꼼히 정리되어 있었다.)
- She neatly organized her itinerary on a piece of paper.
  (그녀는 종이에 일정을 깔끔히 정리해 두었다.)

Pair Work
Practice by substituting the underlined words with other proper words and phrases.

Seunim: Martin, please don't drag your feet when walking.

Martin: Oh, I'm very sorry. I was hurrying and didn't put my shoes on properly.

Seunim: In the temple, all speech, thought, and movement are a part of practice.

Martin: I get it. I should be mindful even when I remove my shoes.

Seunim: Great idea! Don't carelessly toss your shoes aside before entering the building.

Martin: Yes, I'll place them neatly outside the door before I enter.

Unit 4

Anhaeng (Walking in a Single Line)

Anna: After the dawn service, I saw all the seunims form a neat line and walk together in single file.

Seunim: Very good observation! That is called "*anhaeng*."

Anna: *Anhaeng*? What is that?

Seunim: It is called so because it looks as orderly as a flock of geese flying together.

Anna: Oh, so all are walking united in mindfulness!

Seunim: Yes, walking is indeed a part of practice.

Anna: It looked amazing. Watching it made me feel like my mind was becoming orderly and aligned as well.

안행

애나: 오늘 새벽 예불이 끝나고 스님들이 큰방으로 돌아가실 때 한 줄로 질서 정연하게 가시더군요.

스님: 예, 그것을 '안행(雁行)'이라고 합니다.

애나: '안행'이요?

스님: 예, 마치 기러기가 떼를 지어 질서 있게 나는 모습과 같아 그렇게 부르지요.

애나: 그러니까 마음을 챙기며 걸어가시는 거군요.

스님: 예, 걷는 것도 수행이니까요.

애나: 보기가 참 좋았어요. 제 마음도 그렇게 가지런해지는 느낌이었어요.

Words & Phrases

❖ **hold a Buddhist service / chant to the Buddha / worship the Buddha** 예불
- dawn service (새벽 예불)
- 11 a.m. service (사시 예불)
- evening service (저녁 예불)

❖ **look + (형용사) ~보이다**
- All the food looks delicious. (모든 음식이 다 맛있어 보여요!)
- All the children looked very excited. (모든 아이들이 신나 보였어요.)
- The seunims looked peaceful during their meditation. (명상 하시는 스님들은 매우 평온해 보였어요.)

❖ **orderly / aligned / balanced / harmonious** 질서 정연한, 잘 정렬된
- The children formed a line in an orderly fashion. (아이들은 질서 정연하게 한 줄로 섰다.)
- The audience came out of the concert hall in an orderly fashion.
  (관객들은 질서 정연하게 공연장을 빠져 나왔다.)
- He aligned the chairs in straight rows. (그는 의자들을 열을 맞추어 가지런히 해놓았다.)

Pair Work
Practice by substituting the underlined words with other proper words and phrases.

Anna: After the dawn service, I watched as all the seunims formed a neat line to walk in single file.

Seunim: Very good observation! We call that "*anhaeng*."

Anna: *Anhaeng*? What is that?

Seunim: We call it so because it resembles the orderly formation of a flock of geese flying together.

Anna: Oh, so united as they all walk in mindfulness!

Seunim: Yes, walking is indeed a part of practice.

Anna: It looked amazing. Watching them created in me a sense of order and harmony.

Unit 5

Hapjang Banbae
(Pressing One's Palms Together and Making a Half-Bow)

Martin: It looks like there are many monks in this temple.

Seunim: Yes, we have about 30 monks altogether. Some of them work in the temple, and the rest are student monks called "*hagin* seunims."

Martin: What is a *hagin* seunim?

Seunim: A *hagin* seunim is a student monk who attends our monastic college.

Martin: Wow, monks must study hard.

Seunim: Yes. By the way, when you meet monks in the temple, please stop and take a moment to offer a half-bow.

Martin: I know. I have been following that rule diligently.

▶▶ 합장 반배

마틴: 이 도량에 스님이 많으신 것 같아요.

스님: 예, 절에서 소임을 맡은 스님들과 학인 스님들을 합하여 30여 명 됩니다.

마틴: 학인 스님이요?

스님: 예, 저희 승가대학에서 공부하는 학생 스님들을 말합니다.

마틴: 와, 스님들도 공부를 열심히 하시는군요.

스님: 예, 도량 내에서 스님들을 만나면 걸음을 멈추고 합장 반배를 하는 것이 예의입니다.

마틴: 예, 그건 잘 지키고 있습니다.

Words & Phrases

❖ **about** ~정도
- About how many Buddhist temples are there in Korea? (한국에는 사찰이 몇 백 개 정도 있나요?)
- There are about 3,000 sutras stored here. (이곳에는 약 삼천 권의 경전이 보관되어 있습니다.)
- About 3.6 million people live in the city of Busan.
  (부산에는 대략 삼백육십만 명의 사람이 살고 있습니다.)

❖ **mean** 뜻하다, 의미이다
- The word 'seunim' means an ordained Buddhist monk in Korean.
  (스님이란 한국어로 출가한 불교 수도자를 의미한다.)
- The word "hapjang" means a way of greeting to pay respect to seunims.
  (합장은 스님을 뵈었을 때 취하는 행동을 뜻한다.)
- The word "ullyeok" means communal work at temples.
  (운력은 사찰에서 행하는 공동 작업을 뜻한다.)

❖ **monastic college / sangha college** 승가 대학

❖ **take a moment to~** 잠시 시간을 내서 ~을 하다
- We would appreciate it if you would take a moment to fill out the questionnaire.
  (잠시 시간을 내서 설문지를 작성해 주시면 감사하겠습니다.)
- Please take a moment to introduce yourself to the group.
  (잠시 시간을 내서 그룹에 자기소개를 해 주시기 바랍니다.)

❖ **offer** 바치다, 제의하다, (공손히)드리다 (cf. **offering** 공양물)
- The monks made offerings to Buddha. (스님들이 부처님께 공양을 바쳤다.)
- I offered a gift to the abbot. (주지 스님께 가지고 온 선물을 드렸다.)

Pair Work
Practice by substituting the underlined words with other proper words and phrases.

Martin: It seems there are many monks in this temple.

Seunim: Yes, we have about 30 monks altogether. Some work in the temple; the rest are student monks called *"hagin* seunims."

Martin: What is a *hagin* seunim?

Seunim: That refers to student monks attending our monastic college.

Martin: Wow, monks must study hard.

Seunim: Yes. By the way, when meeting monks in the temple, please take a moment to offer a half-bow.

Martin: I know. I follow that rule diligently.

쉬어가는 코너

He, who, is spotless and pure,
Serene and clear like the moon,
Who has destroyed the delight in existence
I call him a holy man.

— *Dhammapada*

티끌 한 점 없이 청정하고
달처럼 고요하고 맑은 사람
세속의 즐거움을 여읜 사람
그런 사람을 성인이라 부른다.

— 법구경

Chapter 5

Lotus Lantern Festival
연등 축제

Unit 1 — The Origin of the Lotus Lantern Festival

Martin: Seunim, it seems there will be many more foreign visitors coming to the Lotus Lantern Festival this year.

Seunim: Yes! I heard the number grows every year.

Martin: What is the history of the Lotus Lantern Festival?

Seunim: Lighting lanterns to celebrate the Buddha's Birthday can be traced back to the Silla period, which is about thirteen hundred years ago.

Martin: How about the Lotus Lantern Festival we see today?

Seunim: That started in 1955 (nineteen fifty-five) at Jogye-sa Temple. When Buddha's Birthday was recognized as a national holiday in Korea in 1975 (nineteen seventy-five), the festival became even larger.

▶▶ 연등 축제의 유래

마틴: 스님, 올해 연등 축제에는 외국인들이 더 많이 참여한대요.

스님: 네, 해마다 외국인의 참여가 증가한다고 들었어요.

마틴: 연등 축제의 유래는 어떻게 되나요?

스님: 부처님오신날에 등을 밝히는 일이 신라시대로부터 시작되었으니 1,300여년의 역사가 있는 셈이지요.

마틴: 그럼 지금과 같은 연등 축제는 언제 시작되었나요?

스님: 1955년 조계사에서 처음 시작되었고 이후 1975년 부처님오신날이 공휴일로 지정되면서 그 규모가 점점 커지게 되었지요.

Words & Phrases

❖ **It seems that/like~** 같습니다
- It seems like every year, more people participate in Templestay programs.
(매년마다 템플스테이 참가자가 늘어나는 것 같습니다.)
- It seems like people from all parts of the world enjoy meditation.
(세계 여러 나라 사람들이 명상을 즐겨 하는 것 같습니다.)
- It seems that prostration practice is becoming popular among young people.
(젊은이들 사이에서 절하는 것이 유행하고 있습니다.)

❖ **the history of~** ~의 역사
- When did the history of Buddhism begin in Korea? (한국 불교의 역사는 언제 시작되었나요?)
- Where does the history of printing in Korea begin? (한국의 인쇄 역사는 어디서 시작되었나요?)

❖ **the Three Kingdoms period** 삼국시대 (**Silla** 신라, **Goguryeo** 고구려, **Baekje** 백제)

❖ **Unified Silla** 통일신라

❖ **be traced back to~ / originate from~ / the origin goes back to~**
~로 거슬러 올라가다, 기원이 ~이다
- That custom can be traced back to the feudal period.
(그 풍습의 기원은 봉건시대에서 찾을 수 있다.)
- Rice farming can be traced back to about BCE 5,000. / The origin of rice farming goes back to about BCE 5,000. (벼농사의 기원은 기원전 5,000년 전으로 거슬러 올라간다.)

Pair Work — Practice by substituting the underlined words with other proper words and phrases.

Martin: Seunim, it seems more foreign visitors shall come to the Lotus Lantern Festival this year.

Seunim: Yes! I witness the number growing every year.

Martin: What's the history of the Lotus Lantern Festival?

Seunim: We can trace the lighting of lanterns to celebrate Buddha's Birthday to the Silla period, about thirteen hundred years ago.

Martin: When did the Lotus Lantern Festival become as we see today?

Seunim: It commenced in 1955 (nineteen fifty-five) at Jogye-sa Temple. Recognized as a national holiday in Korea in 1975 (nineteen seventy-five), the Buddha's Birthday and the festival of lighting lanterns became even larger.

Unit 2: Intangible Cultural Properties

Anna: Seunim, I heard that the Lotus Lantern Festival has been designated as an intangible cultural property.

Seunim: Yes, it was designated as Korea's Important Intangible Cultural Property No.122 in 2012.

Anna: What does 'intangible cultural property' mean?

Seunim: It means the type of cultural asset that does not have a solid form but has great historical or cultural value.

Anna: What are some other examples of important intangible cultural properties in Korea?

Seunim: They include the "Royal Ancestral Rites Music," which is Important Intangible Cultural Property No.1, and Namsadang Nori, which is No.3.

≫ 무형문화재

애나: 스님, 연등회가 무형문화재로 지정되었다고 들었어요.

스님: 예, 2012년에 중요무형문화재 122호로 지정되었습니다.

애나: '무형문화재'는 무엇을 의미하나요?

스님: '형태로 헤아릴 수 없는 문화적인 유산으로서 역사상 또는 예술상 가치가 높은 것'을 의미합니다.

애나: '중요무형문화재'의 예로는 그밖에 무엇이 있나요?

스님: 중요무형문화재 제1호인 종묘제례악, 제3호인 남사당놀이 등이 있지요.

Words & Phrases

❖ **I heard ~** ~들었어요
  - I heard that the scenery is spectacular around the temple in the fall.
    (가을엔 사찰 주변이 정말 아름답다고 들었어요.)
  - I heard that when I go to a temple, I will feel at peace. (절에 가면 마음이 안정될 거라고 들었어요.)

❖ **value** 값어치
  - The value of the Tripitaka Koreana is beyond one's imagination.
    (팔만대장경의 값어치는 감히 매길 수 없습니다.)
  - The value of this experience is priceless. (이번 기회는 매우 값진 것이었습니다.)

❖ **Human Cultural Property** 인간문화재 / **Intangible Cultural Property** 무형문화재 / **National Treasure** 국보

❖ **Namsadang Noli / a multifaceted folk performance tradition originally practiced by travelling entertainers** 남사당놀이

Pair Work
Practice by substituting the underlined words with other proper words and phrases.

Anna: Seunim, I was told the Lotus Lantern Festival was recognized as an intangible cultural property.

Seunim: Yes, it was recognized as Korea's Important Intangible Cultural Property No.122 in 2012.

Anna: What does "intangible cultural property" refer to?

Seunim: It describes the type of cultural property that has no solid form but possesses great historical or cultural value.

Anna: What are some additional examples of Korea's Intangible Cultural Properties?

Seunim: Examples include the royal ancestral rites music, which is Important Intangible Cultural Property No.1. Also, the No.3 property is Namsadang Nori. It is a multifaceted folk performance tradition that was originally practiced by travelling entertainers.

Unit 3

Visiting the Traditional Lantern Exhibit

Martin: Seunim, please hurry! I am dying to see the traditional lantern exhibit.

Seunim: We are almost there. Let's visit the exhibit at Cheonggye-cheon Creek.

Martin: Wow! There are so many beautiful lanterns in different designs and shapes!

Seunim: It is so quaint here. Look at how the lanterns' warm lights are reflected on the water as it flows through the busy downtown of Seoul!

Martin: Seunim, look at this dragon lantern! It looks as if it were alive and breathing!

Seunim: You must be attracted to the dragon because it is your Chinese zodiac sign.

▶▶ 전통 등 전시회 관람

마틴: 스님, 어서 가요. 전통등 전시회를 빨리 보고 싶습니다.

스님: 다 왔어요. 오늘은 청계천 전시회를 보십시다.

마틴: 와, 스님! 정말 등이 예쁘고 모양도 다양하네요.

스님: 도심 안에 이렇게 시냇물이 흐르고 그 주변에 전통 등을 배치해 놓으니 정말 운치가 있네요.

마틴: 스님, 이 용을 보세요. 정말 살아 있는 것 같아요.

스님: 마틴이 용띠라서 용등을 더 좋아하는 것 같군요.

Words & Phrases

❖ **hurry** 서두르다
- Hurry up! (서두르세요!)
- I hurried as much as I could. (최대한 서둘러 왔습니다.)
- Please hurry back. (빨리 돌아와 주세요.)

❖ **almost** 거의
- I am almost at the temple. (절에 거의 다 왔습니다.)
- The registration is almost full. (등록이 거의 다 찼습니다.)
- Dinner is almost ready. (저녁 식사가 거의 다 준비 되었습니다.)

❖ **look alive** 살아 있는 것 같다
- The woman in the painting looked like she was alive. (그림 속의 여자가 살아 있는 것처럼 보였다.)

❖ **Chinese zodiac sign** 띠(태어난 해를 상징하는 열두 동물) / **Western Zodiac sign** 별자리(황도 십이궁)

❖ **quaint** 소담한, 고풍스러운, 운치 있는
- Boppard is a small, quaint town with narrow streets.
  (보파르드는 좁은 거리들로 이루어진 작고 고풍스러운 마을이다.)
- Huy is a quaint market town with a lovely little theatre.
  (후이는 사랑스럽고 작은 극장이 있는, 고풍스러운, 시장이 서는 마을이다.)

Pair Work
Practice by substituting the underlined words with other proper words and phrases.

Martin: Seunim, please come quickly! I am eager to see the traditional lantern exhibit.

Seunim: We are almost there. Let's start by visiting the exhibit at Cheonggye-cheon Creek.

Martin: Wow! It's great to see all the beautiful lanterns in different designs and shapes.

Seunim: It is so quaint here! Look at how the lanterns' warm lights are shining on the water as it flows through the busy downtown of Seoul!

Martin: Seunim, look at this dragon lantern! It looks like it's alive and breathing.

Seunim: The dragons must stand out to you since they are your zodiac sign.

Unit 4

Watching the Lotus Lantern Parade

Anna: I think this is the best spot to watch the lotus lantern parade.

Jackson: Since we got here early, we get to sit down on chairs!

Anna: This is great! Last year, I had to stand, and my feet were hurting so bad.

Jackson: They said the parade starts from Dongdaemun, right?

Anna: Yes, I can't wait till the parade comes to us here at Jongno-3-ga!

Jackson: This is my second year at the festival, and I won't ever forget the experience!

Anna: I agree. Watching so many monks, lay people, students and children marching together in the parade is amazing!

Jackson: Hey, here it comes!

Anna: Wow, each lantern is so unique, and the spectacle of lanterns and thousands of people is amazing!

》》 연등 행렬 관람

애나: 이곳이 연등 행렬을 관람하기에 좋은 장소 같아.

잭슨: 일찍 오니까 의자에 앉아서 볼 수 있네.

애나: 너무 좋아. 작년엔 서서 보느라 다리가 아팠는데…….

잭슨: 행렬이 동대문에서 시작된다고 했지?

애나: 응, 빨리 이곳 종로 3가로 왔으면 좋겠다.

잭슨: 나는 2년째 연등 행렬을 보는데 그 감동은 평생 잊을 수 없을 것 같아.

애나: 그래, 수많은 스님들과 재가자들, 학생들, 어린이들이 참가하더라.

잭슨: 와, 저기 온다!

애나: 다양한 모양의 등이 행렬하는 사람들과 멋진 모습으로 어우러지어져 있네!

Words & Phrases

❖ **ideal / best** 이상적인
- This is the best spot to watch the stars. (별을 보기에 가장 좋은 자리에요.)
- My ideal vacation is to relax and take care of my own well-being.
  (제가 꿈꾸는 휴가란 휴식을 취하면서 건강을 돌보는 것입니다.)

❖ **parade / procession** 행렬
- My favorite part of the festival is the Lotus Lantern Parade.
  (이 축제에서 내가 제일 좋아하는 것은 연등 행렬이야.)

❖ **since** ~이후로, ~부터 (cf. since 는 ~덕분에, ~때문에의 뜻도 있음)
- Since I started to exercise, I feel healthier. (운동을 한 이후로 건강해졌어요.)
- Since 1999, Jack has been a vegetarian. (1999년도부터 잭은 채식주의자가 되었습니다.)
- Cf. Since I got up early, I was able to watch the sunrise.
  (일찍 일어난 덕분에 해돋이를 볼 수 있었어요.)

❖ **start from** ~부터 시작되다
- The line starts here. (줄은 여기서부터 시작됩니다.)
- Preparation for the festival starts from early May. (축제 준비는 5월 초부터 시작합니다.)

❖ **~th year** ~년째 입니다
- This is my first year studying violin. (일 년째 바이올린을 공부하고 있습니다.)
- This is my second year of attending the festival. (축제에 이 년째 참여하고 있습니다.)
- This is my third year of helping my parents. (삼 년째 부모님을 돕고 있습니다.)
- This is my 4th year studying at the university. (4년째 대학에 다니고 있습니다.)

Pair Work
Practice by substituting the underlined words with other proper words and phrases.

Anna: I think this is the best spot to view the lotus lantern procession.

Jackson: Getting here early lets us sit down in chairs!

Anna: Great! Last year, I stood, and my feet hurt badly.

Jackson: Does the procession start from Dongdaemun?

Anna: Yes, I can't wait for the procession to come to us here at Jongno-3-ga!

Jackson: This is my second year at the festival, and I will never forget the experience!

Anna: I agree. To watch so many monks, lay people, students and children marching together in the procession amazes me!

Jackson: Hey, it's coming!

Anna: Wow! Each lantern is unique, and the view of the lanterns and thousands of people is spectacular!

Unit 5

Buddha's Birthday Celebration Ceremony

Anna: This is my first time attending a Buddha's Birthday celebration ceremony.

Martin: It is my first time, too.

Anna: Martin, do you know what year it is in Buddhist Era?

Martin: Yes. In Korea, it is two thousand five hundred fifty-seven in Buddhist Era.

Anna: Wow, you are very knowledgeable! I heard that the Supreme Patriarch of the Jogye Order of Korean Buddhism will be attending today's event.

Martin: I also heard many high-ranking officials from the Korean government, diplomats from foreign missions to Seoul and delegates from other religions will all be attending, too.

▶▶ 봉축법요식

애나: 부처님오신날 봉축법요식은 처음 참석해봅니다.
마틴: 저도 그래요.
애나: 마틴은 올해가 불기 몇 년인지 알아요?
마틴: 네, 한국에서는 불기 2558년이 됩니다.
애나: 와 총명하시군요. 오늘 이곳 조계사 봉축법요식에는 조계종을 대표하는 종정 스님이 참석하신대요.
마틴: 또한 정부, 주한 외교사절, 이웃 종교를 대표하는 분들이 모두 참석하는 성대한 행사라네요.

Words & Phrases

❖ **It / This is the first time** 처음입니다
  - Jeanine, is this your first time at a Templestay? (지닌은 템플스테이에 처음 참여해 본건가요?)
  - This is my first time in Korea. (한국에 처음 와봤어요.)
  - This is my first time experiencing *baru gongyang*. (발우공양은 처음입니다.)
  - Is this your first time trying the lotus position? (가부좌를 처음 해 보았나요?)

❖ **Buddhist Era** 불기
  - The year 2014 is 2558 in Buddhist Era. (2014년은 불기 2558년이다.)

❖ **칭찬의 표현**
  - You are very dexterous / good with your hands! (손재주가 좋으시네요!)
  - You are very good at languages! (언어에 재주가 있으시네요!)
  - You are very knowledgeable about the tea ceremony! (다도에 조예가 깊으시네요!)

❖ **the Supreme Patriarch of the Jogye Order of Korean Buddhism** 종정예하

❖ **VIP / honorary guests / dignitaries** 중요한 손님

Pair Work
Practice by substituting the underlined words with other proper words and phrases.

Anna: I am attending Buddha's Birthday celebration ceremony <u>for the first time</u>.

Martin: It's my first time, too.

Anna: Martin, what year is this in Buddhist Era?

Martin: In Korea, this is two thousand five hundred and fifty-seven in Buddhist Era.

Anna: Wow, you <u>know a lot</u>! I <u>hear</u> that the Supreme Patriarch of the Jogye Order of Korean Buddhism will <u>attend</u> today's event.

Martin: I also <u>hear</u> many <u>high-ranking Korean government officials</u>, diplomats from the foreign missions to Seoul, and <u>other religious delegates</u> will attend as well.

Chapter 6
Ordination and Enlightenment
출가와 해탈

Unit 1 — Getting Ordained as a Buddhist Monk

Martin: Getting ordained as a Buddhist monk seems a life-altering decision.

Seunim: Yes, it means renouncing the mundane world.

Martin: It must be very difficult to cut all ties with one's family.

Seunim: I strongly agree. It is especially difficult to cut the attachment to one's mother.

Martin: However, Buddhist monks have an important goal!

Seunim: Yes, we take a vow to attain enlightenment and save all beings

---

▶▶ 출가

마틴: 출가는 삶에서 매우 중대한 결정일 것 같아요.

스님: 그렇지요. 세속과의 인연을 끊는 일이니까요.

마틴: 가족과의 인연을 끊는 게 쉽진 않을 것 같아요.

스님: 그렇지요, 특히 어머니를 향한 마음을 끊는 게 가장 어렵지요.

마틴: 그래도 원대한 목표가 있잖아요.

스님: 수행하여 깨달음을 얻고 중생을 구제하겠다는 목표가 있지요.

Words & Phrases

❖ **life-altering decision** 인생 최대의 결정
- Leaving my work and coming to Korea was a life-altering decision.
(직장을 그만두고 한국에 오는 건 제 인생 최대의 결정이었어요.)

❖ **renounce the mundane world** 세속과의 인연을 끊다
- Seunim left the mundane world at the age of fifteen.
(스님은 열다섯 살 때 세속과의 인연을 끊으셨습니다.)
- When one wishes to be/become ordained, one must renounce the mundane world.
(출가를 하려면 세속과의 인연을 끊어야 합니다.)

❖ **It must be very difficult to~** 어려운 일일 것 같아요
- It must be very difficult to rise at 3 a.m. (새벽 3시에 일어나는 건 어려운 일일 것 같아요.)
- It must be very difficult to not eat any meat. (고기를 먹지 않는 건 정말 힘들 것 같아요.)

❖ **important goal** 중요한 목표
- For many people, one important goal in life is to have a happy family.
(많은 이들의 인생에서 중요한 목표는 행복한 가정을 꾸리는 것이다.)
- Being healthy is the most important goal for Samantha.
(건강을 지키는 것은 사만다의 가장 중요한 목표입니다.)

❖ **sentient beings** 중생
- May all sentient beings live in peace! (모든 중생이 평화롭기를!)

Pair Work
Practice by substituting the underlined words with other proper words and phrases.

Martin: Ordination as a Buddhist monk is a life-altering decision.

Seunim: Yes, one must renounce the mundane world.

Martin: It must be very difficult to sever contact with one's family.

Seunim: I sincerely agree. It is especially difficult to detach from one's mother.

Martin: However, Buddhist monks have an important purpose!

Seunim: Yes, we vow to attain enlightenment and save all beings.

Unit 2 — The Life of a *Haengja* (Apprentice)

Seunim: When a person decides to become a monk, he or she must start as a *haengja*.

Anna: What is a *haengja*?

Seunim: We could say that it is similar to joining a company as an intern.

Anna: How long do people have to stay as a *haengja*?

Seunim: About six months.

Anna: What do they learn?

Seunim: They learn about Buddha's teachings and get accustomed to the monastic protocol. They also study the text *Admonitions* to *Beginners* or *Chobalsim jagyeongmun*, and attempt to live their lives accordingly.

▶ 행자 생활

스님: 출가를 하면 행자 생활부터 시작하게 됩니다.

애나: '행자'는 무엇을 말하는 것인가요?

스님: 회사로 치면 수습사원 정도라고 할 수 있어요.

애나: 행자 생활은 얼마 동안 하는지요?

스님: 6개월 정도요.

애나: 행자는 무얼 배우나요?

스님: 부처님의 말씀과 사찰의 의례를 익힙니다.
또한 기초적으로 《초발심자경문》을 배우고 그에 따라 삶을 살아갑니다.

Words & Phrases

❖ **apprentice, postulant** 행자
  novice monk (nun) 사미(사미니) / **fully-ordained monk (nun)** 비구(비구니)

❖ **decide to~** ~하기로 결정하다
  - Greg decided to become a monk. (그레그는 스님이 되기로 결심했다.)
  - We decided to meet in front of Jogye-sa at noon tomorrow.
    (우리는 내일 정각에 조계사 앞에서 만나기로 결정했다.)
  - We decided to eat at "Baru Gongyang Restaurant" for lunch.
    (점심에 '발우공양'에 가기로 결정했다.)

❖ **similar / similar to** 비슷하다, 닮았다
  - All roads in the mountains look similar. (산 속의 모든 길은 비슷하게 생겼다.)
  - I look similar to my mother. (저는 어머니를 많이 닮았습니다.)
  - We have similar interests and hobbies. (우리는 비슷한 관심사와 취미 생활을 가졌어요.)

❖ **how long** 얼마나
  - How long is this program? (이 프로그램은 기간이 얼마나 걸리나요?)
  - How long does it take from Seoul to Miso-sa Temple? (서울에서 미소사까지 얼마나 걸리나요?)
  - How long will you be gone? (얼마 동안 자리를 비우시나요?)

❖ **get accustomed to / get used to** 익숙해지다
  - It took a while to get accustomed to the subway system in Seoul.
    (서울의 전철 시스템에 익숙해질 때까지 꽤 오랜 시간이 걸렸다.)
  - You will get accustomed to the new environment in no time.
    (금방 새로운 환경에 익숙해질 거예요.)

❖ **Admonitions to Beginners / the text to encourage beginners to arouse the aspiration to attain enlightenment** 초발심자경문 / 초심자에게 깨달음을 얻겠다는 발원을 하도록 독려하는 책

Pair Work Practice by substituting the underlined words with other proper words and phrases.

Seunim: <u>After deciding</u> to become a monk, a person must start as a *haengja*.

Anna: <u>What's a</u> *haengja*?

Seunim: We could say that <u>it's like joining</u> a company as an intern.

Anna: <u>For how</u> long <u>are</u> people a *haengja*?

Seunim: <u>Close</u> to six months.

Anna: What <u>do</u> they <u>learn</u>?

Seunim: They <u>learn</u> about Buddha's teachings and monastic protocol. They also <u>study</u> the text called the *Chobalsim jagyeongmun*, which <u>means</u> "the text to encourage beginners to arouse the aspiration to attain enlightenment" while attempting to live their lives accordingly.

Unit 3

Monastic College (Sangha College)

Anna: After the *haengja* stage, does one become a seunim?

Seunim: Yes. A man becomes a *sami*, a novice monk, and a woman becomes a *samini*, a novice nun, after receiving his or her novice ordination.

Anna: Are there any further steps?

Seunim: Yes, they study for four more years. Traditionally, they would attend a monastic college or practice Seon at a special Seon center called Gicho Seonwon.

Anna: Are there the untraditional routes?

Seunim: Yes, ordained novice monks and nuns can study at Central Sangha University or at Dongguk University.

▶▶ 승가대학

애나: 행자 생활을 잘 마친 사람은 스님이 되나요?

스님: 예, 계를 받고 사미 또는 사미니가 됩니다.

애나: 다음 단계도 있나요?

스님: 네, 이후 4년 동안 공부를 합니다. 전통적으로는 승가대학에서 공부를 하거나 기초선원에서 선 수행을 합니다.

애나: 전통적이 아닌 경우는요?

스님: 중앙승가대학교나 동국대학교에서 4년간 공부를 하지요.

Words & Phrases

❖ **after** 뒤에, 후에
- After the Templestay, I will go back to Britain. (템플스테이가 끝나면, 저는 영국으로 돌아갑니다.)
- After my meditation, I would like to go for a walk. (명상 후에 산책을 하고 싶어요.)
- I will go to the movies after finishing my daily tasks.
  (오늘 일을 마치고 난 후에 영화를 보러 가겠어요.)

❖ **novice ordination** 사미(사미니)계

❖ **steps / stages / phases / process** 단계, 과정
- What are the necessary steps to make *gimchi*? or What is the process for making *gimchi*?
  (김치를 담그려면 어떠한 과정을 거쳐야 하죠?)
- What are the steps to become a doctor? (의사가 되려면 어떤 단계를 완수해야 하나요?)

Pair Work
Practice by substituting the underlined words with other proper words and phrases.

Anna: After the *haengja* phase, does one become a seunim?

Seunim: Yes. A man becomes a *sami*, a novice monk, and a woman a *samini*, a novice nun, after receiving the novice ordination.

Anna: Are there any further steps?

Seunim: Yes, they study for four more years. Traditionally, they attend Sangha University or practice Seon at a special Seon center called Gicho Seonwon.

Anna: Are there some unconventional routes?

Seunim: Ordained novice monks and nuns can study at Central Sangha University or Dongguk University.

Buddhist Practice as a Seunim

Seunim: After completing four years of study, one will receive full ordination as a *bigu*, a monk, or a *biguni*, a nun.

Anna: Does that finally make a person a fully-pledged Buddhist monk?

Seunim: Yes. Whereas novice monks and nuns, *samis* and *saminis*, receive 10 precepts, fully ordained monks, *bigus*, must follow two hundred fifty precepts, and fully ordained nuns, *bigunis*, must follow three hundred forty-eight precepts.

Anna: One can say that if *sami* and *samini* are beginner seunims, *bigu* and *biguni* are official seunims!

Seunim: You are correct! They are now committed to fulfill their vow to attain enlightenment and save all beings. Therefore, they must practice by meditating or studying the Buddhist canon of Tripitaka.

Anna: What kind of Buddhist practice do you mainly do in Korea?

Seunim: Our practice is called Ganwha Seon.

▶▶ 수행

스님: 4년간의 공부를 마친 사람은 비구계 혹은 비구니계를 받습니다.

애나: 이제 정식 스님이 된 건가요?

스님: 그렇지요. 사미 · 사미니는 10계를 받고 비구는 250계, 비구니는 348계를 받아 지닙니다.

애나: 사미 · 사미니가 초보 스님이라면 비구 · 비구니는 정식 스님이군요.

스님: 이제부터는 삼장 공부나 참선 수행 등을 통해 깨달음을 얻고 중생을 제도할 수 있도록 노력해야 합니다.

애나: 한국에서는 주로 어떤 수행을 하는지요?

애나: 간화선 수행을 합니다.

Words & Phrases

❖ **Ganwha Seon** 간화선

❖ **attain enlightenment** 깨달음을 얻다
- Seunims perform rigorous practice every day to attain enlightenment.
(스님들은 매일 깨달음을 얻기 위해 용맹 정진 하신다.)

❖ **save all beings** 중생을 제도하다
- Every morning, the sound of seunims chanting to save all sentient beings resonates throughout the mountains. (매일 아침, 중생을 제도하려는 스님들의 불공 소리가 산세에 울려 퍼진다.)

❖ **fully-pledged Buddhist monk / full-fledged Buddhist monk** 정식 스님
- What does it take to become a full-fledged Jogye Order monk?
(정식 조계종 스님이 되려면 어떻게 해야 하나요?)

Pair Work
Practice by substituting the underlined words with other proper words and phrases.

Seunim: Having studied for four years, one receives full ordination as a *bigu*, a monk, or a *biguni*, a nun.

Anna: Is the person then a fully-fledged Buddhist monk?

Seunim: Yes. While novice monks and nuns, *samis* and *saminis*, follow 10 precepts, fully-ordained monks, *bigus*, must obey two hundred fifty precepts, and fully ordained nuns, *bigunis*, must follow three hundred forty-eight precepts.

Anna: You might say that *bigu* and *biguni* are official seunims whereas *sami* and *samini* are beginner seunims!

Seunim: Correct! They pledge to attain enlightenment and to save all beings. Therefore, they are to practice through meditation or study of the Buddhist canon of Tripitaka.

Anna: What kind of Buddhist practice is common in Korea?

Seunim: We call our practice Ganwha Seon.

Unit 5

Liberation

Anna: Seunim, what does it mean to be "liberated?"

Seunim: It means attaining enlightenment. One leaves the cyclical existence of samsara and enters Nirvana.

Anna: Does that mean the ultimate goal for seunims is to reach enlightenment?

Seunim: That is true. However, in Mahayana Buddhism, we do not distinguish between saving all beings and reaching enlightenment.

Anna: How does one know if one has reached enlightenment?

Seunim: One must receive the approval of an enlightened master.

해탈

애나: 스님, '해탈'이란 무엇을 의미합니까?

스님: '깨달음을 얻는다.' 즉 윤회의 세계에서 열반의 세계로 가는 것을 말합니다.

애나: 그럼 스님들이 수행하시는 궁극적인 목적이 깨달음인가요?

스님: 물론 그렇긴 하지만 대승불교에서는 중생을 교화하는 것과 깨달음을 얻는 것을 둘로 나누지 않습니다.

애나: '깨달음'의 경지에 이르렀는지는 어떻게 압니까?

스님: 선지식께 점검을 받아야 합니다.

Words & Phrases

❖ **be liberated / liberation** 해탈
- Jim shared many conversations about being liberated with seunim.
(짐은 해탈에 대하여 스님과 많은 대화를 나누었다.)

❖ **attain enlightenment** 깨달음을 얻다
- Lauran learned that attaining enlightenment means to escape the world of samsara and reach Nirvana. (로렌은 깨달음을 얻는 것이 윤회의 세계에서 열반의 세계로 가는 것임을 배웠다.)

❖ **different matter / separate / separated** 각기 다른 일
- Practicing and being mindful are not two different matters.
(수행과 마음 챙기기는 각기 다른 일이 아닙니다.)
- This food and I are not separate. We are connected.
(나와 이 음식은 각기 다르지 않습니다. 우리는 하나입니다.)

❖ **receive approval from an enlightened teacher** 선지식인으로부터 인가를 받다

Pair Work
Practice by substituting the underlined words with other proper words and phrases.

Anna: Seunim, what does it signify to be "liberated?"

Seunim: It signifies "attaining enlightenment." In this state, one leaves the cyclical existence of samsara and enters Nirvana.

Anna: Is the ultimate goal for seunims to reach enlightenment?

Seunim: That is the goal. However, in Mahayana Buddhism, we aren't distinguishing saving all beings and reaching enlightenment as two unconnected matters.

Anna: How does one know if one has reached enlightenment?

Seunim: One has to receive acknowledgement from an enlightened master.

쉬어가는 코너

Ancient Thoughts

– Cheongheo Hyujeong

Though the winds are dormant, the flowers fall.
The mountains become more poignant with the singing of birds.
The sky and white clouds awaken together
While the water and radiant moon flow in harmony.

고의

– 청허휴정(淸虛休靜, 1520~1604)

古意

바람은 자건만 꽃은 오히려 지고
새 우는 소리에 산은 더욱 그윽하다
하늘은 흰 구름과 함께 새는데
물은 밝은 달과 섞여 흐른다

風定花猶落
鳥鳴山更幽
天共白雲曉
水和明月流

Chapter 7

Etiquette with Foreign Participants for Seunims to Remember 스님이 외국인에게 지켜야 할 예절

Unit 1 How to Address Westerners on a First-Name Base

Anna: Seunim, Westerners prefer to be addressed by their first names.

Seunim: Really?

Anna: Yes. By the way, you kindly address me by my first name, "Anna," but other seunims don't.

Seunim: Is calling someone by his or her first name such an important matter?

Anna: Yes. We address each other by our first names from the time when we are very small children until we become adults. Even married couples call each other by their first names!

Seunim: I see the cultural difference.

Anna: During Templestays, I wish we would be addressed by our first names. It will be easy since we all have name tags on!

▶▶ 이름 부르기

애나: 스님, 서양인들은 이름을 불러주는 것을 좋아합니다.

스님: 그래요?

애나: 스님께서는 저를 '애나'라고 불러주시지만 다른 스님들은 안 그러세요.

스님: 이름 부르는 게 그렇게 중요해요?

애나: 네, 저희는 아주 어려서부터 성인이 되어 직장에 취직할 때까지 이름을 부르지요. 또 부부 간에도 서로 이름을 불러요.

스님: 문화가 다르군요.

애나: 템플스테이를 할 때도 저희 이름을 불러주면 좋겠어요. 이름표도 착용하고 있으니 쉽잖아요.

Words & Phrases

❖ **prefer** 선호하다
- They preferred to be called "seunim" rather than by their names.
  (스님들께선 성함보다는 스님이라 불러드리는 걸 좋아하세요.)
- I prefer to sit in the front. (저는 앞에 앉는 걸 선호하는 편입니다.)
- What do you prefer to do? (어떻게 했으면 좋겠나요?)

❖ **the case / the situation / the circumstance** 실정, 사실
- In many cases, foreign tourists do not get to experience Korea's traditional culture.
  (많은 외국 관광객들이 한국의 전통문화를 경험하지 못하는 것이 사실입니다.)
- That's not the case in Korea. (한국의 실정은 그렇지 않아요.)

❖ **address** 주소(명사), 지목하다, 부르다(동사), 문제를 다루다(동사)
- What is the address of Jogye-sa Temple? (조계사 주소가 어떻게 되나요?)
- How should we address you? (존함을 어떻게 부르면 되나요?)
- I addressed that issue yesterday, and I solved the problem. (어제 그 문제를 다루어 시정했습니다.)

❖ **name tags** 명찰

Pair Work
Practice by substituting the underlined words with other proper words and phrases.

Anna: Seunim, Westerners <u>like to be called by</u> their first names.

Seunim: Really?

Anna: Yes, you kindly address me by my first name "Anna" but <u>that's</u> not the case with other monks.

Seunim: Is calling someone by his or her first name <u>so crucial</u>?

Anna: Yes. We <u>call</u> each other by our first names from <u>childhood to adulthood</u>. Even married couples call each other by their first names!

Seunim: I see the cultural difference.

Anna: During Templestays, <u>I'd like to</u> be addressed by my first name. It will be easy since we have name tags on!

Unit 2 Introducing Oneself

Martin: Seunim, how about if we take a moment to introduce ourselves?

Seunim: Hmm. We have a very busy schedule. Would that be necessary?

Martin: Because we will be spending the next two days together, I think we should get to know one another.

Seunim: Sure. Would you like to go first, Martin? If you wish, perhaps you can tell us your name, what you do for a living and your reason for participating in this Templestay.

Martin: Yes, Thank you. I would like to introduce myself by starting. …

Seunim: Wow, after introducing each other, I think everyone feels more comfortable. What a great idea!

▶▶ 자기소개

마틴: 스님, 먼저 각자 자기소개를 하면 어떨까요?

스님: 오늘 일정이 좀 바쁜데 꼭 자기소개가 필요해요?

마틴: 저희들은 이틀 동안 함께 지낼 예정이잖아요. 그렇다면 서로에 대해 좀 알아야 한다고 생각합니다.

스님: 그래요. 그럼 마틴부터 간단히 자기소개를 해보세요. 이름과 현재 하고 있는 일, 그리고 이 행사에 참가하게 된 동기 정도를 말하면 되겠네요.

마틴: 네, 감사합니다. 그럼 제 소개를 시작하겠습니다. …

스님: 와, 자기소개를 하고 나니까 분위기가 훨씬 부드러워졌네요. 아주 좋습니다!

Words & Phrases

❖ **How about if ~?** 어떨까요?
  - How about if we go to the Dharma hall first? (먼저 법당에 가보는 것이 어떨까요?)
  - How about if you go to your dormitory and unpack your luggage?
    (먼저 숙소에 가서 짐을 푸는 것이 어떨까요?)
  - How about if we take turns using the water fountain? (차례대로 식수대를 사용하면 어떨까요?)
  - How about if we start off by stretching first? (시작하기에 앞서, 스트레칭을 하면 어떨까요?)
  - How about if we feed the children first? (아이들부터 음식을 주는 것이 어떨까요?)

❖ **Is that a must?** 꼭 해야 하나요?

❖ **Would that be necessary? / Is that necessary?** 그게 필요한가요?

❖ **get to know ~ / get acquainted with ~** 좀 더 알아가다
  - I want to get to know about Korea while I am here. (내가 여기 있는 동안 한국에 대해 알고 싶다.)
  - I got to know more about Buddhism. (불교를 더욱 알게 되었다.)
  - I got acquainted with Sam through Templestay. (템플스테이를 통해 샘을 알게 되었어요.)

❖ **breaking the ice** 서로를 알기 위한, 서먹함을 풀기 위한
  - After the game, the ice was broken and everyone started to interact with each other.
    (게임을 끝내자 서먹함이 풀려 모든 이들이 서로 어울리기 시작했다.)

Pair Work

Practice by substituting the underlined words with other proper words and phrases.

Martin: Seunim, may we briefly introduce ourselves?

Seunim: Hmm. We have a very busy schedule. Is that necessary?

Martin: Because we are spending the next two days together, I think we should become acquainted.

Seunim: Sure. Care to go first, Martin? If you wish, perhaps you can share your name, what you do for a living and your reason for participating in this Templestay.

Martin: Not at all. Thank you. I would like to introduce myself by stating.

Seunim: Wow, after breaking the ice, I think everyone feels more comfortable around each other. What a great idea!

Unit 3 Accommodating Participants' Needs during Meditation

Seunim: We will now start meditation. So please have a seat on the floor in a half-lotus position as you have just learned.

Anna: Seunim, I cannot sit on the floor for a long time because my legs hurt too much. May I sit on a chair instead?

Seunim: No problem! I have prepared chairs in the back for just such people.

Anna: Thank you very much for your understanding.

Seunim: I respect that every individual is different. Sitting on a chair may even help you focus better.

Anna: I feel so relieved that you are not scolding me for not being able to sit in the lotus position.

▶▶ 좌선에 대한 배려

스님: 지금부터 참선을 시작하겠습니다. 좀 전에 배운대로 반가부좌를 하고 앉으십시오.

애나: 스님, 저는 다리가 아파 바닥에 오래 앉을 수가 없어요. 혹시 의자에 앉아서 해도 될까요?

스님: 당연하지요. 그런 분이 계실까봐 저 뒤에 의자도 준비해 두었습니다.

애나: 너무 고맙습니다.

스님: 개인차를 존중하는 것입니다. 그리고 의자에서 수행해도 집중을 잘 할 수 있습니다.

애나: 가부좌를 못한다고 나무라지 않으시니 마음이 편합니다.

Words & Phrases

❖ **We will now start + (명사 / 동명사)** 지금부터 시작하겠습니다
  - We will now start the first day of our Templestay. (지금부터 템플스테이 첫째 날을 시작합니다.)
  - We will now start tonight's concert. (지금부터 오늘 저녁 콘서트의 막을 열겠습니다.)
  - We will now start today's performance. (이제 오늘 공연을 선보이겠습니다.)
  - We will now start meditation class. (이제 명상 수업을 시작하겠습니다.)
  - We will now start eating breakfast. (지금 우리가 아침 식사를 시작하겠습니다.)
  - Have a seat, grab a seat, take a seat. (앉아 주세요.)
  - Please have a seat on the cushion. (방석 위에 앉아 주세요.)
  - Grab a seat on a chair please. (의자에 앉아 주세요.)
  - Please take a seat in the front row first. (가장 앞자리부터 앉아 주세요.)

❖ **too much** 너무나
  - It hurts too much. (너무나 아파요.)
  - I ate too much. (너무 많이 먹었어요.)
  - I guess I walked too much. (너무 많이 걸었나 봐요.)

❖ **difference** 차이
  - difference of opinion (견해의 차이)
  - cultural difference (문화적 차이)
  - age difference (나이 차이)

Pair Work

Practice by substituting the underlined words with other proper words and phrases.

Seunim: We will now start to meditate. So please sit on the floor in a half-lotus position as you learned.

Anna: Seunim, I can't sit on the floor long since my legs are hurting. May I sit on a chair instead?

Seunim: No problem! I have prepared chairs in the back for such cases.

Anna: Thank you very much for your tolerance.

Seunim: I recognize individuals are different. To sit on the chair may even assist you to focus more.

Anna: I'm relieved that you aren't scolding me for not sitting in a lotus position.

Unit 4 — Respecting Each Individual's Decisions

Martin: Seunim, Christine said that because she is Christian, she would rather not attend the Dharma service.

Seunim: You are all here to experience Korea's traditional culture and temple life. However, you do not have to attend the service if you feel it is against your religion.

Martin: Is it okay to stay in the back and observe quietly?

Seunim: Yes, of course! Now, let's go have tea with our abbot. But I believe I don't see Kevin.

Martin: Seunim, Kevin wishes to have some quiet time alone. He said he would stay in his room.

Seunim: I understand. It is okay as long as you can keep your mind calm and focused, no matter what you choose to do.

선택의 문제

마틴: 스님, 크리스틴은 기독교도라서 예불에 참석하기 어렵다고 합니다.

스님: 여러분은 한국의 전통문화와 사찰 문화를 체험하러 오신 겁니다. 하지만 예불을 종교의식이라 여기신다면 참석하지 않아도 좋아요.

마틴: 뒤에서 조용히 참관만 하는 것도 괜찮겠지요?

스님: 괜찮습니다. 자 이제 주지 스님과 차담을 나누러 갈까요? 그런데 케빈이 안보이네요?

마틴: 스님, 케빈은 조용히 자기 시간을 좀 더 가지고 싶답니다. 그래서 그냥 방에 남아 있습니다.

스님: 예, 무엇을 하든 자기 마음을 돌아보고 고요히 할 수 있으면 됩니다.

Words & Phrases

❖ **rather / a little / a bit / a little bit** 꽤, 약간
- It's rather late to call my aunt. (이모님께 전화 드리기엔 꽤 늦은 시간이네요.)
- You are a bit overweight. (약간의 과체중이십니다.)

❖ **rather than** ~보단 ~이 낫다
- Because of her Buddhist beliefs, Vivian chose a faux fur coat rather than a real fur coat.
  (비비안은 자신의 불교적 믿음을 지켜 진짜 모피코트 대신 가짜 모피코트를 골랐다.)
- I would rather go to a temple in the mountains than a busy vacation spot.
  (복잡한 휴가지 보다 산속에 있는 사찰에 가겠습니다.)

❖ **wish to ~ / want to ~ / desire to ~** 하고 싶어 하다
- He wishes to extend his stay at the temple. (그는 사찰에 더 머물고 싶어 한다.)
- David wishes to learn temple cuisine. (데이비드는 사찰 음식을 배우고 싶어 한다.)
- Sandra wishes to visit Beopju-sa with her family. (산드라는 가족과 법주사에 가고 싶어 한다.)

❖ **no matter what** 비록 무엇이 ~일지라도, ~한다 하더라도
- No matter what you do, please come to the Dharma hall by 4 a.m.
  (어떤 일이 있을지라도, 대웅전에 오전 4시까지 오세요.)
- No matter what others say, listen to your own heart.
  (다른 이들이 뭐라 하더라도 자신의 마음에 귀를 기울이세요.)

Pair Work
Practice by substituting the underlined words with other proper words and phrases.

Martin: Seunim, because she is Christian, Christine would rather not attend the Dharma service.

Seunim: You are all here to learn Korea's traditional culture and temple life. However, don't feel compelled to attend the service if you feel it's against your religion.

Martin: May I stay in the back and observe quietly?

Seunim: Yes, of course! Now, let's go have tea with our abbot. But I haven't seen Kevin.

Martin: Seunim, Kevin desires some quiet time alone. He said he would remain in his room.

Seunim: I understand. Keep your mind calm and focused, no matter what you choose to do.

Unit 5

Acceptance

Anna: Seunim, I initially thought that when I visited a temple, I would feel very relaxed and comfortable.

Seunim: Why did you think so?

Anna: Because Buddha is the great man with endless compassion and monks are his followers.

Seunim: Yes, you are indeed right.

Anna: However, when we got together for the first time yesterday, I did not feel accepted. Instead, I felt my presence here was not welcome.

Seunim: What do you think made you feel that way?

Anna: I think it was because you were very strict from the beginning. You started by reciting the rules and explaining temple etiquette, telling us what to do and what not to do.

Seunim: How would you like to have it differently?

Anna: On the first day, I wish to hear you say things like, "Relax and rest your mind" or "Let go of all your worries." Also, I think it is important to have the participants introduce themselves and get to know each other a little better.

Seunim: They are great ideas. I will make sure to implement them in the future. Thank you, Anna!

▶▶ 포용

애나: 스님, 저는 절에 오면 참 편안할 것이라고 생각했어요.
스님: 왜 그렇게 생각했어요?
애나: 부처님은 자비심이 가득한 분이시잖아요. 그리고 스님들은 그런 부처님을 따르는 제자들이고요.
스님: 그런데요?
애나: 그런데 어제 저희들이 모였을 때 포용보다는 무언가 접근을 차단한다는 느낌이 들었어요.
스님: 왜 그런 느낌이 들었을까요?
애나: 처음부터 너무 딱딱한 분위기에서 이것은 해서는 안 되고 저것도 해서는 안 된다, 사찰 예절을 잘 지켜라 등등의 말씀만 하셨잖아요.
스님: 그럼 어떻게 하면 더 좋았겠어요?
애나: 우선 하루 이틀 동안은 "마음을 푹 쉬어라.", "걱정을 내려놓아라." 등의 말을 듣고 싶었어요. 그리고 참가자들끼리 자기소개를 해서 서로를 좀 알면 좋겠어요.
스님: 좋은 의견이니 적극 수용하겠습니다. 감사합니다.

Words & Phrases

❖ **initially** 처음에, 당초에
- Initially, I signed up for a 2-day program. (처음엔 1박 2일 프로그램을 신청했어요.)
- Initially, many people assume that the Templestay program will be boring.
(많은 사람들이 처음엔 템플스테이 프로그램이 지루할 거라 생각해요.)

❖ **loving-kindness and compassion** 자애와 자비
- Metta meditation cultivates loving-kindness. (자비관은 자애심을 닦는다.)
- Budhisattvas practice compassion in their daily lives. (보살은 나날의 삶에서 자비를 행한다.)

❖ **strict** 엄격한
- The monk in charge of the retreat is very strict and uptight.
(입승 스님이 아주 엄격하고 깐깐하셔요.)
- The rules are too strict. There are no exceptions allowed.
(규칙이 너무 엄합니다. 예외가 전혀 허용되지 않아요.)

❖ **How can +** (대명사) + (동사)? 어떻게 하면?
- How can we make it better? (어떻게 하면 더 좋을까요?)
- How can we improve this program? (프로그램을 어떻게 개선시킬 수 있을까요?)
- How can we share Korean Buddhism with all the people around the world?
  (어떻게 한국의 불교를 전세계에 알릴 수 있을까요?)

❖ **let go of / put down / relinquish** 내려놓다
- Let go of your worries. (걱정을 내려놓으세요.)
- Let go of your thoughts. (생각을 내려놓으세요.)
- Put down your bag here. (가방을 여기에 내려놓으세요.)

Pair Work
Practice by substituting the underlined words with other proper words and phrases.

Anna: Seunim, I initially believed visiting a temple would relax and comfort me.

Seunim: Why did you believe so?

Anna: Because Buddha has endless compassion and monks are his followers.

Seunim: Yes, you are correct.

Anna: However, when we met for the first time yesterday, I did not experience acceptance. Instead, I felt unwelcomed.

Seunim: Why did you feel that way?

Anna: I think you were very strict from the beginning.
You related the rules and temple etiquette, sharing with us what to do and what not to do.

Seunim: How would you like to have it differently?

Anna: On the first day, you might say things like, "Relax and rest your mind" or "Let go of all your worries." Also, I think participants should introduce themselves and get to know each other a little better.

Seunim: Those are great ideas. I intend to implement them in the future. Thank you Anna!

Ox-Herding

– Soyo Taeneung

The ox roams and pastures lie east and west of the stream.
Flowery grasses are abundant and water shimmers far away.
Why bother haltering and tying up the beast
When not a single one into another's plot goes astray?

목우행
　　– 소요 태능(逍遙太能, 1562~1649)

소를 놓아먹이는 시내 이쪽저쪽에
꽃다운 풀 우거지고 물은 길이 흐르는데
등등하나 남의 농사 침범하지 않거니
어찌 구태여 고삐로 꼭 잡아 매어 두리

牧牛行

溪潤東西放牧牛
萋萋芳草水悠悠
騰騰不犯他家苗
何必繩頭繫把留

Part 2

Buddhist Tenets and Practices

불교 교리와 수행

- Chapter 1 **The Ethics of Buddhism** 불교의 윤리

- Chapter 2 **The Teachings from the Scriptures and the Recorded Sayings of Sages** 경전과 어록의 가르침

- Chapter 3 **Seon Practice in Korea** 한국의 선수행

Chapter 1: The Ethics of Buddhism

불교의 윤리

Unit 1: Ten Unwholesome Deeds (十惡業; *Sibageop*)

Of the many unwholesome activities we commit in daily life, the ten unwholesome deeds (十惡業) are committed in body, speech, and mind. If we repent of these ten unwholesome deeds and act in the completely opposite way, we can perform the ten wholesome deeds (十善業). Of the ten unwholesome deeds, unwholesome words are the most common. Considering that the *Thousand Hands Sutra* begins with the "mantra for purification of speech (淨口業眞言)," we should begin to consider how many times we speak unwholesome words every day. The ten unwholesome deeds are as follows.

1) Killing, the act of taking life (殺生)
2) Stealing, the act of taking what is not yours (偸盜)
3) Sexual misconduct, committing immoral sexual acts (邪婬)
4) Lying, the act of saying what is not true (妄語)
5) Ornate speech, the act of engaging in pointless or flattering speech (綺語)
6) Insult, the act of engaging in abusive or derogatory speech (惡口)
7) Slander, the act of saying things to alienate or hurt people (兩舌)
8) Covetousness, being envious of what others have (貪欲)
9) Anger, to be consumed with hatred and loathing over perceived wrongs (瞋恚)
10) False views, to believe in false or wrong views (邪見)

The ten unwholesome deeds are further divided into three categories. First, in the category of "deeds caused by bodily action (身業)," there are killing, stealing, and sexual misconduct. Second, in the category of "deeds caused by speech (口業)," there are lying, double talk, insult, and slander. Third, in the category of "deeds caused by one's mind (意業)," there are covetousness, anger, and false views.

십악업(十惡業)

우리가 살아가며 짓는 많은 악업 가운데 신·구·의 삼업에 해당되는 열 가지가 바로 십악업이다. 이 십악업을 참회하고 정반대로 행하게 되면 결국 십선업이 된다. 십악업 중에서도 일상생활에서 흔히 범하기 쉬운 것이 바로 구업이다. 《천수경》의 맨 처음 구절이 '정구업진언'으로 시작되는 것으로 미루어 보아도 입으로 짓는 업이 얼마나 많은지를 짐작할 수 있다. 십악업은 다음과 같다.

1) 생명을 죽이는 살생.
2) 타인의 소유물을 훔치는 투도.
3) 간음으로 남녀의 도덕을 문란하게 하는 사음.
4) 사실이 아닌 것을 말하는 망어.
5) 실없고 잡된 말을 하는 기어.
6) 말로써 욕하거나 멸시하는 악구.
7) 이간질하는 양설.
8) 욕심에서 벗어나지 못하는 탐욕.
9) 잘못되었다고 생각하는 것에 대해 증오나 혐오에 빠지는 진에.
10) 그릇된 견해에 빠지는 사견 또는 우치를 말한다.

이 십악업 중 살생(殺生)·투도(偸盜)·사음(邪淫)은 신업(身業)에, 망어(妄語)·기어(綺語)·악구(惡口)·양설(兩舌)은 구업(口業)에, 그리고 탐욕(貪慾)·진에(瞋恚)·사견(邪見)은 의업(意業)에 속한다.

Fill in the Blanks

❖ 1. The ten unwholesome deeds are committed in _____, speech, and mind. (신, 몸)

❖ 2. If we _____ of these ten unwholesome deeds and act in the completely opposite way, we can perform the ten wholesome deeds. (참회하다)

❖ 3. The "mantra for _____ of speech (정구업진언)"

❖ 4. Killing, the act of taking _____ (살생)

❖ 5. _____, the act of taking what is not yours (투도)

❖ 6. _____, the act of engaging in abusive or derogatory speech (악구)

❖ 7. _____, to be consumed with hatred and loathing over perceived wrongs (진에)

part 2. Buddhist Tenets and Practices

❖ 8. First, in the category of "deeds caused by bodily action (신업)," there are killing, stealing, and sexual _____. (잘못된 행동)

❖ 9. Second, in the category of "deeds caused by speech (구업)," there are lying, ornate speech, insult, and _____. (양설, 중상)

❖ 10. Third, in the category of "deeds caused by one's mind (의업)," there are _____, anger, and false views. (탐욕)

Questions

1. How do we commit the ten unwholesome deeds?
2. What is the most common way of committing the ten unwholesome deeds?
3. Is covetousness committed by bodily action?
4. What are the four unwholesome deeds caused by speech?
5. Of the three categories of unwholesome deeds, where does anger belong?

Unit 2

The Verse of the Common Teaching of the Seven Buddhas (七佛通偈; *Chilbultongge*)

In the sense that it is the verse taught by all seven Buddhas of the past, it is called *"The Verse of the Common Teaching of the Seven Buddhas."* This verse is found in two Chinese scriptures: the *Sutra of the Appearance of Light* (出曜經) and the *Dharmapada* (法句經).

> Not to commit a single unwholesome action, but to do all that is wholesome.
> To cultivate a pure mind — this is the teaching of all Buddhas.

Unwholesome actions exert unwholesome influences on self and others. Unwholesomeness refers to the three basic afflictions of greed, anger, and ignorance. Greed arises from attachment to what one likes while anger arises from opposition to what one hates. Anger makes one unable to see things in the proper perspective. Ignorance refers to being foolish and without much wisdom.

"Wholesomeness" refers to a state where unwholesomeness is expunged. It also means that one's mind is free of greed, anger, and ignorance. Buddhism places importance on the issues of "wholesomeness and unwholesomeness" because of its concern with putting belief into practice. All sentient beings have Buddha nature, and thus, they can become Buddhas by attaining enlightenment. They attain Buddhahood by cleansing and purifying their minds. Whenever greed, anger, or ignorance arises in one's mind, one should fill their mind with generosity, loving-kindness, and wisdom.

칠불통게(七佛通偈)

과거에 있었던 일곱 부처님이 한결같이 설한 게라는 뜻에서 칠불통게라고 부른다. 이 게는 초기경전의 《출요경》과 《법구경》에 나온다.

> 모든 그릇된 악을 짓지 말고, 여러 가지 선한 일을 받들어 행하라.
> 스스로 마음을 깨끗하게 하면, 이것이 모든 부처님의 가르침이니라.
> 諸惡莫作 衆善奉行 自淨其意 是諸佛敎

'악'은 자신과 남에 대해 좋지 못한 영향을 끼치는 것으로서 탐·진·치 삼독심을 뜻한다. '탐'이란 좋아하는 것에 대한 집착에서 생기고, '진'이란 싫어하는 것을 배척하여 분노를 일으켜 그 결과 올바른 가치 판단을 하지 못하는 상태를 말한다. '치'란 지혜가 없는 어리석음을 말한다.

선은 악이 제거된 상태로 내 마음에 탐·진·치가 없는 것을 말한다. 불교에서 선악을 중요시하는 것은 실천의 문제가 뒤따르기 때문이다. 모든 중생은 불성을 가지고 있으며 깨달음을 통해 부처가 될 수 있다. 부처가 되는 방법은 스스로 그 마음을 맑히는 것이다. 매 순간 올라오는 탐욕·성냄·어리석음을 관용·자애·지혜로 가득 채우는 것이다.

Fill in the Blanks

❖ 1. "*The Verse of the Common Teaching of the Seven Buddhas*" is found in two Chinese _____. (경전)

❖ 2. To _____ a pure mind — this is the teaching of all Buddhas. (닦다)

❖ 3. Unwholesome actions _____ unwholesome influences on self and others. (발하다, 끼치다)

❖ 4. Unwholesomeness refers to the three basic _____ of greed, anger and ignorance. (번뇌)

❖ 5. Greed arises from _____ to what one likes while anger arises from opposition to what one hates. (집착)

❖ 6. Anger makes one unable to see things in the proper _____. (관점)

❖ 7. Ignorance refers to being _____ and without much wisdom. (어리석은)

❖ 8. Buddhism _____ importance on the issues of "wholesomeness and unwholesomeness." (두다)

❖ 9. Because of its concern with putting belief into _____ (실천)

❖ 10. They attain Buddhahood by _____ and purifying their minds. (씻어내다)

Questions

1. Is *Chilbul tongge* found in the Chinese scripture *Dharmapada?*
2. What does "unwholesomeness" refer to?
3. Does anger lead one to better insight of circumstances?
4. Why does Buddhism place importance on the issues of "wholesomeness and unwholesomeness?"
5. Do sentient beings attain Buddhahood by purifying their minds?

Unit 3 — The *Uposatha* (布薩; *Posal*)

The *uposatha* (Skt. *upavasatha*) is a ceremony of repentance observed by each monastic sangha twice a month, on the 15th and 29th (or 30th) days. On those days, all monastics from each sangha get together. First, they recite the *Code of Vinaya Precepts* (Pali *patimokkha*, Skt. *prātimokṣa*). With the recitation of each precept, any member who has violated that particular precept comes forward and repents in front of the whole group. When the question about whether there was a violation or not of each precept is asked three times, and there is silence, then it means that there has been no violation of that particular rule.

The purpose of *uposatha* is to help monastics maintain a life based on the precepts and to remember them all. Therefore, it is important to hold the *uposatha* regularly with proper intervals in between. For *uposatha* to be effective, it must be based on mutual trust among the members. Also required is the courage to confess one's wrongs in front of others and a mindset to be able to repent with utmost sincerity. In addition, members need to exhibit loving-kindness and generosity in order to accept others' wrongs without regarding them as weaknesses.

포살(布薩)

승가에서 보름마다 한 번씩, 즉 15일과 29일(또는 30일)에 집단적으로 행하는 참회를 말한다. 이때에는 현전 승가에 속한 모든 출가인이 다 모인다. 포살은 먼저 함께 계법을 외우고 한 계목을 외울 때마다 어긴 적이 있는 이는 스스로 대중 앞에서 참회하는 의식이다. 세 번을 거듭 물었을 때 모두 가만히 있으면 모인 대중이 그 계에 대하여 청정하다는 것을 의미한다.

포살의 목적은 정기적으로 계목을 낭송함으로써 계를 잊지 않고 계에 기반한 생활을 할 수 있도록 하기 위함이다. 따라서 포살은 적절한 간격으로 정기적으로 하는 것이 중요하다. 포살이 제대로 되려면 상호 신뢰가 바탕이 되어야 하며 대중 앞에서 자신의 잘못을 드러낼 수 있는 용기와 지극한 마음으로 참회할 수 있는 마음이 필요하다. 또한 타인의 잘못을 약점으로 삼지 않고 받아주는 사랑과 관용이 있어야 한다.

Fill in the Blanks

❖ 1. The _____ is a ceremony of repentance observed by each monastic sangha twice a month. (포살)

❖ 2. On *uposatha* days, all _____ from each sangha get together. (스님들)

❖ 3. With the recitation of each precept, any member who has violated that particular precept comes forward and _____ in front of the whole group. (참회하다)

❖ 4. When the question about whether there was a _____ or not of each precept is asked three times (위반)

❖ 5. The purpose of *uposatha* is to help monastics maintain a life _____ ____ the precepts and to remember them all. (기반한)

❖ 6. Therefore, it is important to hold the *uposatha* regularly with proper _____ in between. (간격)

❖ 7. For *uposatha* to be effective, it must be based on _____ _____ among the members. (상호 신뢰)

❖ 8. Also required is the courage to _____ one's wrongs in front of others. (고백하다)

❖ 9. Also required is a _____ to be able to repent with utmost sincerity. (마음 자세)

❖ 10. In addition, members need to exhibit loving-kindness and _____ in order to accept others' wrongs without regarding them as weaknesses. (관용)

Questions

1. How often does a monastic sangha observe the *uposatha*?
2. How many times is the question about whether there was a violation or not of each precept asked at the *uposatha* ceremony?
3. What is the purpose of *uposatha*?
4. Is *uposatha* effective when there is lack of trust among the members?
5. Besides trust, what else is needed for the effective observance of *uposatha*?

Unit 4

The *Pavāraṇā* (自恣; Jaja)

The *pavāraṇā* (Skt. pravāraṇā) is a ceremony of repentance performed at the end of each meditation retreat. At this ceremony each individual asks the others if he did any wrong during the retreat, and the retreat participants respond and discuss the matter for the benefit of the one who asked. During the time of the Buddha, the *pavāraṇā* was performed once a year, but in Korea, it is performed twice a year at the end of the summer and winter meditation retreats.

For *pavāraṇā* to be beneficial, when others point out your flaws, you must be able to accept their comments without anger or bad feelings. In addition, when you point out the flaws of others, it should be based on concern and affection without any hint of attack or blame. Therefore, to perform *pavāraṇā*, one must be willing to ask others about one's own faults with a humble mind and embrace what others say. In addition, those who point out another's faults must speak with a compassionate mind and without being confrontational; they must speak without any distinction between "you" and "I," as if speaking to themselves. This system will not work without a foundation of mutual trust.

▶▶ 자자(自恣)

자자는 안거가 끝나는 날 자신의 허물을 대중에게 묻고 대중은 그를 위하여 허물을 말해주는 참회법이다. 부처님 당시에는 1년에 1번 자자를 했지만 하안거, 동안거를 하는 한국에서는 연 2회 자자를 행한다. 자자가 잘 행해지기 위해서는 다른 사람이 잘못을 지적해 줄 때 분노나 서운함 없이 그대로 받아들일 수 있어야 하고 또 다른 사람의 잘못을 지적할 때도 공격이나 비난이 아닌 애정과 관심을 바탕으로 해야 한다. 그러므로 자자를 하기 위해서는 먼저 겸손한 마음으로 다른 사람에게 자신의 허물을 물을 수 있어야 하고, 다른 사람이 지적해 주는 것을 그대로 받아들일 수 있어야 하며, 지적하는 사람 또한 나와 너의 대립감 없이 바로 자신에게 말하듯이 자비의 마음으로 잘못을 일깨워 주어야 한다. 이는 상호 신뢰가 바탕이 되지 않으면 결코 이루어질 수 없는 제도이다.

Fill in the Blanks

❖ 1. The *pavāraṇā* is a ceremony of repentance performed at the end of each _____ _____. (안거)

❖ 2. At this ceremony each individual asks the others if he did _____ _____ during the retreat. (잘못)

❖ 3. During the time of the Buddha, the *pavāraṇā* was performed _____ a year. (한 번)

❖ 4. For *pavāraṇā* to be _____, when others point out your flaws, you must be able to accept their comments without anger or _____ _____. (유익한, 악감정)

❖ 5. In addition, when you point out the flaws of others, it should be based on _____ and affection without any hint of attack or _____. (관심, 비난)

❖ 6. Therefore, to perform *pavāraṇā*, one must be willing to ask others about one's own faults with a _____ _____. (겸손한 마음)

❖ 7. In addition, those who point out another's faults must speak with a compassionate mind and without being _____. (대립하는)

Questions

1. When is the *pavāraṇā* ceremony performed?
2. How often was the *pavāraṇā* performed during the time of the Buddha?
3. When others discuss your flaws at the *pavāraṇā*, how should you take them?
4. When you point out the faults of others, what is the proper frame of mind?

Unit 5

Repentance (懺悔; *Chamhoe*)

Practitioners must be willing to change themselves. The first signal of this change is repentance for the wrongs one has committed in the past. And if one truly desires to change, this repentance also applies to any wrongs one may commit in the present and in the future. Repentance is to regret one's wrongs wholeheartedly, understand the root cause of those wrongs, and not repeat them ever. Thus, with genuine repentance, there are no wrongs beyond expiation.

Though Angulimala killed 999 people, he became an arhat because of his deep regret and repentance. The karma from unwholesome actions vanishes when one repents, but it multiplies when one tries to conceal them. Thus, no matter how trifle a wrong may be, you should eradicate it with repentance. If not, all one's wrongs accumulate to pose a hindrance to successful practice. Therefore, do not think about repentance as being difficult. Pay respect to Buddha by prostrating yourself in front of him and confess your wrongs sincerely. Then reflect deeply to understand why you committed the wrong so that you won't do it again.

▶▶ 참회(懺悔)

수행자는 첫째 자신을 바꾸려는 자세가 필요하다. 그 변화의 첫 신호가 지금까지 자신이 저질러온 잘못에 대한 참회이다. 또한 그대로 살아갔더라면 현재는 물론 앞으로도 계속해서 저질러졌을 잘못에 대한 참회이다. 참회란 잘못에 대해 크게 뉘우치고 그 잘못의 근본 원인까지 알아서 다시는 그러한 잘못을 반복하지 않는 것이다. 따라서 진정한 참회를 할 때 속죄하지 못할 죄가 없다. 앙굴리말라는 999명의 사람을 죽이고도 깊이 뉘우치고 참회했으므로 아라한이 될 수 있었다. 죄는 참회하면 사라지지만 감추면 더욱 커지므로 아무리 작은 잘못이라도 참회하여 그 뿌리를 끊어야 한다. 그렇지 않으면 이런 죄업이 모두 쌓여서 수행에 큰 장애가 된다. 그러므로 참회를 어려워하지 말고 부처님 전에 엎드려 예배하고 진심으로 잘못을 고할 일이다. 그런 다음 잘못의 원인이 어디에 있었는지를 깊이 살펴서 다시는 그러한 잘못을 반복하지 않도록 해야 할 것이다.

Fill in the Blanks

- 1. Practitioners must be willing to _____ themselves. (변화하다)
- 2. The first _____ of this change is repentance for the wrongs one has committed in the past. (신호)
- 3. And if one truly _____ to change, this repentance also applies to any wrongs one may commit in the present and in the future. (원하다)
- 4. Repentance is to regret one's wrongs _____, understand the root cause of those wrongs, and not repeat them ever. (진심으로)
- 5. Thus, with genuine repentance, there are no wrongs beyond _____. (속죄)
- 6. The karma from unwholesome actions _____ when one repents. (사라지다)
- 7. The karma from unwholesome actions multiplies when one tries to _____ them. (감추다)
- 8. Thus, no matter how _____ a wrong may be, you should eradicate it with repentance. (사소한, 작은)
- 9. If not, all one's wrongs accumulate to pose a _____ to successful practice. (장애)
- 10. Pay respect to Buddha by prostrating yourself in front of him and confess your _____ sincerely. (잘못)

Questions

1. Does repentance signify one's willingness to change?
2. Does repentance only involve regretting one's past wrongs wholeheartedly?
3. Are there any wrongs that cannot be expiated?
4. Does the karma from unwholesome actions vanish when one doesn't repent?
5. Why is repentance important for one's practice?

Unit 6

The Three Refuges (三歸依戒; *Samgwi-uigye*), the Five Precepts (五戒; *Ogye*), the Ten Precepts (十戒; *Sipgye*), and the Precepts for Bhikkhus and Bhikkhunis (比丘·比丘尼戒; *Bigu-gye & Biguni-gye*)

The "three refuges" (三歸依戒) refer to taking refuge in the "Three Jewels of Buddhism": the Buddha, the Dharma, and the Sangha. They represent one's belief that the Buddha, his teachings, and the Sangha are the most precious jewels in the world, and it is an expression of one's vow to walk the path of truth by relying on nothing but the three jewels. The first step as a Buddhist is to commit oneself to the three refuges. Therefore, all Buddhist ceremonies begin with committing to the three refuges. To take refuge in the three jewels is to make one's foundation of faith solid. Without strong faith, one cannot attain the fruit of the Buddhist path. To make a vow of this solid faith is the three refugees.

The five precepts (五戒) are: to refrain from taking life (不殺生), to refrain from stealing (不偸盜), to refrain from sexual misconduct (不邪淫), to refrain from false speech (不妄語), and to refrain from intoxicants (不飮酒). The five precepts constitute the foundation of all the other precepts. Of the five precepts, especially important are the first four because violating them harms others. If ordained monks and nuns violate any one of those four, that is, if they kill a human being, steal, engage in sexual misconduct, or lie about their spiritual attainments, they have committed one of the "four grave offenses (四波羅夷; pārājika)." The four grave offenses are not tolerated by the Buddhist order. Thus, those who have committed one of those four will be defrocked and expelled from the Sangha. On the other hand, taking intoxicants is not an offense by itself, but the first four precepts are easily violated under the influence of intoxicants. That's why it has become one of the five precepts.

The ten precepts (十戒) are also called "precepts for novices (沙彌戒; *samigye*)" as they are observed by novice monks (沙彌; *śrāmaṇera*; Kr. *sami*) and nuns (沙彌尼; *śrāmaṇerī*; Kr. *samini*). "*Sami* (沙彌)" is a transliteration of the Sanskrit "*śrāmaṇera*," which means "to cease from unwholesome deeds and do works of compassion (息慈)." In other words, it means to cease from being influenced by the secular world and to save sentient beings through compassion. The ten precepts are as follows.

1. Refrain from killing (不殺生; *pāṇātipātāveramaṇi*)
2. Refrain from stealing (不偷盜; *adinnādānāver*)
3. Refrain from sexual misconduct (不邪婬; *abrahmacaryaver*)
4. Refrain from false speech (不妄語; *musāvādāver*)
5. Refrain from intoxicants (不飲酒; *suramereyya-majjapamādaṭṭhānāver*)
6. Refrain from eating at improper times (不非時食; *vikāla-bhojanāver*)
7. Refrain from watching or engaging in dancing, singing, and performances (不歌舞觀聽; *nacca-gīta-vādita-visūkadassanāver*)
8. Refrain from adorning oneself with garlands, perfumes, and ointments (不塗飾香鬘; *mālā-gandha-vilepana-dhāraṇa-maṇḍana-vibhūṣanaṭṭhānā*)
9. Refrain from sleeping on an elevated bed (不坐高廣大牀; *uccāsayanā-mahāsayanā*)
10. Refrain from having gold and silver (不蓄金銀寶; *jātarūpa-rajata-paṭiggahaṇāver*)

Novices are eligible to receive bhikkhu or bhikkhuni precepts after completing a training course of four years. Bhikkhu or bhikkhuni precepts provide a gateway to become full-fledged monks or nuns as well as virtues to practice throughout one's lifetime. The novices who have passed screening test take a 10-day training course. Upon its completion, novice monks receive 250 precepts to become bhikkhus while novice nuns take 348 precepts to become bhikkhunis.

삼귀의계(三歸依戒), 오계(五戒), 십계(十戒), 비구·비구니계(比丘·比丘尼戒)

삼귀의란 삼보에 귀의한다는 의미다. 즉 부처님과 부처님의 가르침과 승가가 이 세상에서 가장 뛰어난 보배라는 것을 믿겠다는 것이며, 삼보 외의 다른 것에 의지하지 않고 오직 불·법·승 삼보에 귀의함으로써 진리의 길에 들겠다는 서원이다. 불자의 시작은 삼귀의에 있기에 모든 의식에서는 맨 먼저 삼귀의례를 한다. 삼보에 귀의한다는 것은 믿음의 뿌리를 확고히 하는 것이다. 믿음을 굳건히 하지 않으면 불도수행의 열매를 얻을 수 없다. 이러한 굳은 믿음을 맹세하는 것이 삼귀의다.

오계는 살생하지 않고(不殺生), 도둑질하지 않고(不偸盜) 사음하지 않고(不邪淫), 거짓말하지 않으며(不妄語), 술 마시지 않는 것(不飮酒)을 말한다. 오계는 모든 계의 근본이다. 오계 중에서 살생·투도·음행·망어는 특히 중요하여 출가자가 이를 범한 경우 4바라이죄가 된다. 즉 출가자가 사람을 죽이거나, 물건을 훔치거나, 음행을 하거나, 자신이 이른 수행 수준에 대해 거짓말을 한다면, 이는 용인할 수 없는 대죄로 간주되어 출가자의 자격을 박탈당하고 승가에서 방출되는 벌을 받는다. 반면 음주는 그것 자체로는 죄가 되지 않지만 음주로 인해 앞의 모든 계를 어길 수 있기 때문에 역시 오계의 하나가 되었다.

십계는 사미·사미니가 지켜야 할 계율이라는 뜻에서 사미계라고도 부른다. 사미(śrāmaṇera)는 범어를 소리 나는 대로 표기한 것으로 그 뜻은 '쉬고 자비한다(息慈)', 즉 '나쁜 일을 쉬고 자비를 행한다'는 의미이다. 이것은 세간에 물드는 일은 쉬고 중생을 자비로 제도한다는 것이다. 십계는 아래와 같다.

첫째, 살아있는 것을 죽이지 마라.
둘째, 훔치지 마라.
셋째, 음행하지 마라.
넷째, 거짓말 하지 마라.
다섯째, 술 마시지 마라.
여섯째, 때 아닌 때에 먹지 마라.
일곱째, 노래하고 춤추고, 풍류 잡히지 말며, 가서 구경하지도 마라.
여덟째, 꽃다발을 쓰거나 향을 바르지 마라.
아홉째, 높고 큰 평상에 앉지 마라.
열째, 금이나 은 등의 보물을 가지지 마라.

비구·비구니계는 사미·사미니가 4년의 교육 과정을 거친 후 받을 수 있다. 비구·비구니계는 정식 스님이 되는 관문인 동시에 평생을 실천해야 할 덕목이다. 자격 심사에 합격한 사미·사미니는 10일 간의 연수를 받는다. 이후 비구는 250계 비구니는 348계를 받는다.

Fill in the Blanks

❖ 1. The "three refuges" refer to taking refuge in the "_____ _____ of Buddhism." (삼보)
❖ 2. They represent one's _____ that the Buddha, his teachings, and the Sangha are the most precious jewels in the world. (믿음)
❖ 3. It is an expression of one's _____ to walk the path of truth by relying on nothing but the three jewels. (서원)
❖ 4. Therefore, all Buddhist ceremonies begin with _____ ____ the three refuges. (전념하다, 헌신하다)
❖ 5. To take refuge in the three jewels is to make one's foundation of faith _____. (확고한, 단단한)
❖ 6. Without strong faith, one cannot attain the _____ of the Buddhist path. (열매)
❖ 7. The five precepts constitute the _____ of all the other precepts. (근본)
❖ 8. If ordained monks and nuns violate any one of those four, they have committed one of the "four _____ _____." (중죄, 바라이죄)
❖ 9. The four grave offenses are not _____ by the Buddhist order. (용인하다)
❖ 10. Thus, those who have committed one of these four will be _____ and expelled from the Sangha. (성직을 박탈당하다)
❖ 11. The first four precepts are easily violated under the _____ of intoxicants. (영향)
❖ 12. The ten precepts are also called "precepts for _____" as they are observed by novice monks and nuns. (사미승)

Questions

1. What are the three refuges?
2. Why do all Buddhist ceremonies begin with taking the three refuges?
3. Can one attain the fruit of the Buddhist path without a strong faith?
4. Is refraining from intoxicants one of the five precepts?
5. Do the four grave offenses include taking intoxicants?
6. Why are the ten precepts also called "precepts for novices?"
7. If you eat at improper times, are you observing the ten precepts?

Chapter 2 The Teachings from the Scriptures and the Recorded Sayings of Sages 경전과 어록의 가르침

Unit 1

The *Heart Sutra*
(般若心經; Skt. Prajñāpāramitā-hṛdaya; Kr. Banya simgyeong)

The *Heart Sutra* is the most often recited sutra at Korean Dharma assemblies and Buddhist services. Consisting of 260 Chinese characters, it is a short sutra that succinctly explains the main points of the *Mahāprajñāpāramitā Sūtra*.

The core concept of the *Heart Sutra* is emptiness (空; Skt. *śūnyatā*). The true nature of all phenomena is emptiness. In essence, the sutra says: "Phenomena (dharma) are devoid of permanent substance. All things change ceaselessly."

> Form does not differ from emptiness,
> Emptiness does not differ from form.
> Form itself is emptiness; emptiness itself is form.
> So too are feeling, perception, mental formations, and consciousness.

Dealing with "form" and "emptiness," the *Heart Sutra* espouses the "Middle Way," the heart of the Buddha's teachings. The sutra neither negates form in its affirmation of emptiness, nor does it negate emptiness in its affirmation of form, thus integrating form and emptiness. In addition, neither the *Heart Sutra* nor Buddhist doctrine expounds that nothing exists; in other words, they don't teach the negative understanding of emptiness called "nihilistic emptiness (斷滅空)."

반야심경(般若心經)

《반야심경》은 한국에서 법회나 예불을 올릴 때 가장 많이 독송하는 경전이다. 《대반야바라밀다경》의 요점을 간략하게 설명한 짧은 경전으로, 총 260자로 되어 있다.

《반야심경》의 핵심은 '공(空)'이다. 일체법의 참다운 모습은 공이라는 것이다. 다시 말해서 "만물은 고정된 실체가 없다. 모든 것은 끝없이 변화한다."는 것을 이렇게 표현한다.

> 색이 공과 다르지 않고
> 공이 색과 다르지 않으며,
> 색이 곧 공이요 공이 곧 색이니,
> 수·상·행·식도 그러하니라.

《반야심경》에는 또한 부처님의 가르침의 핵심인 중도가 들어 있다. 공을 말하면서도 색을 부정하지 않고 색을 말하면서도 공을 부정하지 않아 이를 종합하기 때문이다. 참고로 《반야심경》이나 부처님 말씀 전체는 '아무 것도 없음' 즉 '단멸공'을 말하지 않는다.

Fill in the Blanks

❖ 1. The *Heart Sutra* is the most often _____ sutra at Korean Dharma assemblies and Buddhist services. (독송되는)

❖ 2. Consisting of 260 Chinese _____, it is a short sutra that succinctly explains the main points of the *Mahāprajñāpāramitā Sūtra*. (글자)

❖ 3. The core concept of the *Heart Sutra* is _____. (공)

❖ 4. The _____ _____ of all phenomena is emptiness. (실상)

❖ 5. In essence, the sutra says: "Phenomena (dharma) are _____ of permanent substance. (없는)

❖ 6. All things change _____. (부단히)

❖ 7. Form does not _____ _____ emptiness. (다르다)

❖ 8. The *Heart Sutra* espouses the "Middle Way," the _____ of the Buddha's teachings. (핵심)

❖ 9. The sutra does not _____ form in its affirmation of emptiness. (부정하다)

❖ 10. In addition, neither the *Heart Sutra* nor Buddhist _____ expounds that nothing exists. (교리)

Questions

1. What is the most often recited sutra at Korean Dharma assemblies?
2. How many Chinese characters are in the *Heart Sutra*?
3. What is the core concept of the *Heart Sutra*?
4. According to the *Heart Sutra*, does form differ from emptiness?
5. Does the *Heart Sutra* affirm nihilistic emptiness?

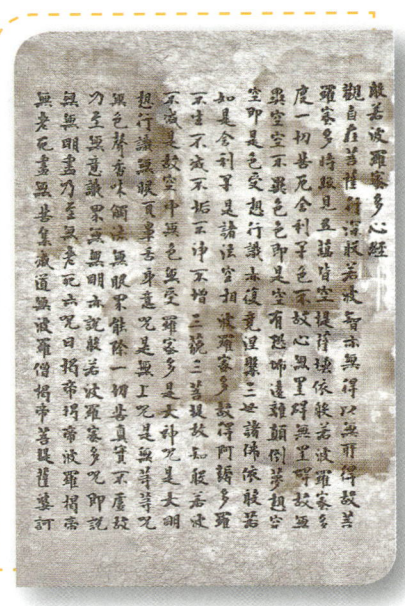

Unit 2

The *Diamond Sutra*
(金剛經; Ch. *Jingang jing*; Kr. *Geumgang gyeong*)

The *Diamond Sutra* is much revered by Korean Buddhists as a foundational sutra of the Jogye Order of Korean Buddhism. Its Korean title *Geumgang gyeong* (金剛經) is condensed from its fuller title *Geumgang banya baramil gyeong* (金剛般若波羅蜜經; Skt. *Vajracchedikā-prajñāpāramitā Sūtra*). Its pithy text is thought to express the basic concepts of Mahayana Buddhism. It belongs to the Prajñāpāramitā (般若部) category of scriptures. The Buddha taught the content of this sutra at the Jetavana Monastery in Śrāvastī.

The *Diamond Sutra* is presented as a dialogue between the Buddha and Subhūti. It says that all things, including the world of perception, are void of substance and self-nature and that all things (and people) are intrinsically empty and without an inherent self. It is said that the Sixth Patriarch Huineng attained great awakening upon hearing the passage from this sutra which says, "Let the mind arise without dwelling on anything (應無所住 而生其心)."

The *Diamond Sutra* is a Mahayana text which was compiled in India about 500 years after the Buddha entered nirvana. It was first translated into Chinese by Kumārajīva (鳩摩羅什) in the 5th century. Of the many versions rendered by different translators, that of Xuanzang (玄奘) is also well known along with that of Kumārajīva. Ever since its first translation, many virtuous teachers have written commentaries to clarify the text, and as a result, various commentaries on the *Diamond Sutra* exist. During the time of the Sixth Patriarch, more than 800 commentaries were said to exist.

One of the most often recited passages from the *Diamond Sutra* is the four-line verse below.

> Things that arise and cease from all conditioned phenomena
> Are like dreams, illusions, bubbles, shadows,

Dew, and lightning.
Such is how one should contemplate and observe.

The Jogye Order's Institute of Buddhist Studies published the *Standard Diamond Sutra of the Jogye Order (Jogyejong pyojun geumgang gyeong)* in 2009. This was an effort to overcome the undesirable situation where devotees were reciting from different versions of the *Diamond Sutra* because there were so many versions of Chinese and Korean text. Researchers compared different versions of the Chinese translation of the *Diamond Sutra* for two years and collated them with the Sanskrit version from which the Chinese version was translated. In this way, they tried to reflect the original meaning of the sutra and express it in modern Korean language.

금강경(金剛經)

대한불교조계종의 소의경전으로서 한국 불자들에게 많은 사랑을 받고 있는 《금강경》은 《금강반야바라밀경》의 줄인 이름으로, 대승불교의 기본 사상을 함축적으로 표현하고 있는 경전이다. 반야부에 속하는 이 경전은 부처님께서 사위국 기원정사에서 설한 가르침이다. 수보리와의 대화 형식으로 이어지는 가르침은 인식의 세계 등 모든 것은 물거품처럼 실체가 없고, 자성이 없고(無自性), 공(空)이며 무아(無我)임을 설하고 있다. 특히 육조혜능이 이 경전의 "응무소주 이생기심(應無所住 而生其心)"이라는 말을 듣고 대오했다고 한다.

부처님 열반 후 500여 년이 지나 인도에서 편찬된 대승경전인 《금강경》은 5세기에 구마라집에 의해 최초로 한역되었다. 그밖에 7세기에 번역한 현장의 한역본이 다수의 번역본 중에서도 알려져 있다. 이후 그 뜻을 정확하게 이해하기 위하여 수많은 선지식들이 해석을 했고, 그 결과 오늘날 수많은 《금강경》의 해석본들이 전해진다. 육조혜능 당시만 해도 800여 종이 넘었다고 한다. 《금강경》 중에서도 널리 애송되는 사구게는 다음과 같다.

일체 현상계의 모든 생멸법은 꿈과 같고 환상과 같고
물거품과 같고 그림자 같으며 이슬과 같고 번개와도 같으니
응당 이와 같이 관해야 한다.
　一切有爲法 如夢幻泡影 如露亦如電 應作如是觀

2009년 조계종 불학연구소에서는 《조계종 표준 금강경》을 발간했다. 이는 다양한 한문본과 한글 번역본이 있어 불자들이 각기 다른 《금강경》을 독송하는 폐단을 극복하기 위한 것이었다. 2년 동안 금강경의 한문 번역본들을 비교하고 금강경 편찬 당시의 산스크리트어와 대조하면서 원뜻을 바르게 새기는 한편 용어도 현대어로 맞추는 작업을 한 결과물이다.

Fill in the Blanks

❖ 1. The *Diamond Sutra* is much revered by Korean Buddhists as a _____ _____ of the Jogye Order of Korean Buddhism. (소의경전)

❖ 2. Its Korean title *Geumgang gyeong* (금강경) is _____ from its fuller title *Geumgang banya baramil gyeong*. (축약되다)

❖ 3. Its pithy text is thought to express the _____ _____ of Mahayana Buddhism. (기본 개념)

❖ 4. The Buddha taught the content of this sutra at the _____ _____ in Śrāvastī. (기원정사)

❖ 5. The *Diamond Sutra* is presented as a _____ between the Buddha and Subhūti. (대화)

❖ 6. The Sixth Patriarch _____ attained great awakening upon hearing the passage from this sutra. (혜능)

❖ 7. Let the mind arise without _____ on anything. (머물다)

❖ 8. It was first _____ _____ Chinese by Kumārajīva (구마라십) in the 5th century. (번역되다)

❖ 9. Since its first translation, many virtuous teachers have written _____ to clarify its text. (논서)

❖ 10. One of the most often recited passages from the *Diamond Sutra* is the _____ verse below. (사구)

❖ 11. This was an effort to _____ the undesirable situation where devotees were reciting from different versions of the *Diamond Sutra*. (극복하다)

❖ 12. Researchers _____ different versions of the Chinese translation of the *Diamond Sutra* for two years. (비교하다)

Questions

1. Why is the *Diamond Sutra* important to the Jogye Order of Korean Buddhism?
2. Does the *Diamond Sutra* express the basic concepts of Theravada Buddhism?
3. Where did the Buddha teach the content of this sutra?
4. In the *Diamond Sutra*, who is the dialogue between?
5. Which passage inspired the Sixth Patriarch Huineng to attain great awakening?
6. Who first translated the *Diamond Sutra* into Chinese?
7. Why did the Jogye Order publish the *Standard Diamond Sutra of the Jogye Order* in 2009?

Unit 3

Verses on the Mind of Faith (信心銘; Ch. Xinxin ming)

Written by the Third Patriarch Sengcan, *Verses on the Mind of Faith* is fondly recited at Seon temples. It is a rather short text, consisting of 148 phrases in 592 characters with four characters in each phrase. However, it is said to contain all the essentials of both the Seon and Doctrinal Schools. *Verses on the Mind of Faith* also espouses the Middle Way, a basic concept of Buddhism. As such it is recognized as one of the greatest records of Seon School, along with the *Platform Sutra*.

The heart of *Verses on the Mind of Faith* is the "Middle Way which is free from the two extremes." It is a terse representation of the Middle Way devoid of the relative concepts sentient beings hold in their daily lives, concepts such as love and hate, right and wrong, or like and dislike. Ven. Seongcheol referred to *Xinxin ming* as a "comprehensive exposition on the Middle Way" and praised the text by saying, "I marvel at how it expresses the Middle Way so simply and with such beautiful language, a concept the Buddha taught all his life." Following is an excerpt from *Xinxin ming*.

> The Supreme Way is not difficult
> If only you do not discriminate.
> When love and hate are both bereft,
> You will clearly understand.
> Make the smallest distinction,
> And you are as far apart as heaven from earth.
> If you wish to see the truth,
> Hold no opinions for or against anything.

신심명(信心銘)

삼조 승찬대사가 저술한 《신심명》은 예로부터 선종 사찰에서 애송되어 왔다. 사언절구의 시문형식으로서 148구 592자로 구성된 짧은 책이지만 선과 교의 핵심을 다 담았다고 한다. 《신심명》은 또한 불교의 근본 사상인 중도가 담겨져 있어 혜능대사의 《육조단경》과 더불어 선종 최고의 어록으로 인정받고 있다.

《신심명》의 근본 핵심은 '양변을 여읜 중도'라 할 수 있다. 미워함과 사랑함[憎愛], 옳음과 그름[是非], 좋아함과 싫어함[好惡] 등 일상생활에서 나타나고 있는 중생의 상대 개념을 떠난 중도법을 간명하게 표현한 것이다. 성철스님은 '신심명은 중도 총론'이라 하며 "부처님께서 한평생 말씀하신 중도를 어떻게 이렇게 아름다운 언어로 간단명료하게 잘 설명했는지 모르겠다"고 극찬하였다. 다음은 《신심명》의 일부분이다.

지극한 도는 어렵지 않음이요 오직 간택함을 꺼릴 뿐이니
미워하고 사랑하지만 않으면 통연히 명백하니라.
털끝 만큼이라도 차이가 있으면 하늘과 땅 사이로 벌어지나니
도가 앞에 나타나길 바라거든 따름과 거슬림을 두지 마라.
至道無難 唯嫌揀擇 但莫憎愛 洞然明白
毫釐有差 天地懸隔 欲得現前 莫存順逆

Fill in the Blanks

❖ 1. Written by the Third _____ Sengcan, *Verses on the Mind of Faith* is fondly recited at Seon temples. (조사)

❖ 2. However, it is said to contain all the _____ of both the Seon and Doctrinal Schools. (핵심, 요체)

❖ 3. *Verses on the Mind of Faith* also espouses the _____ _____ , a basic concept of Buddhism. (중도)

❖ 4. As such it is recognized as one of the greatest records of _____ _____, along with the *Platform Sutra*. (선종)

❖ 5. The heart of *Verses on the Mind of Faith* is the "Middle Way which is free from the _____ _____." (양변)

❖ 6. It is devoid of the _____ concepts sentient beings hold in their daily lives. (상대적)

❖ 7. Ven. Seongcheol referred to *Xinxin ming* as a "_____ exposition on the Middle Way." (종합적인)

❖ 8. I _____ _____ how it expresses the Middle Way so simply and with such beautiful language. (찬탄하다)

❖ 9. The _____ _____ is not difficult if only you do not discriminate. (지극한 도)

❖ 10. When love and hate are both _____, you will clearly understand. (여읜, 상실한)

❖ 11. Make the smallest _____, and you are as far apart as heaven from earth. (구별)

❖ 12. If you wish to see the truth, hold no _____ for or against anything. (견해)

Questions

1. Why is the *Xinxin ming* fondly recited at Seon temples?
2. Who is the author of the *Verses on the Mind of Faith*?
3. What is the core concept of the *Verses on the Mind of Faith*?
4. Did Ven. Seongcheol praise the *Verses on the Mind of Faith*?
5. According to *Xinxin ming*, what do you need to do if you wish to see the truth?

Unit 4

Song of Enlightenment (證道歌; Ch. *Zhengdao ge*)

The *Song of Enlightenment* (證道歌: Kr. *Jeungdo-ga*) is a Seon collection of verse that describes the attainment of enlightenment. "Jeung (證)" refers to the enlightened state, "do (道)" the truth all people must put into practice, and "ga (歌)" a poem in which sound and rhythm are gracefully harmonized. It is said to have been composed by the Tang Dynasty Seon Master Yongjia Xuanjue (永嘉玄覺; 675–713) on the day after his enlightenment was confirmed by the Sixth Patriarch Huineng. It describes one's state of mind after attaining great enlightenment and is written in the style of old Chinese verse. It contains 266 phrases in 1,814 characters. It is thought to have been written in the early 8th century.

As one of the masterworks of the Seon School, along with the *Xinxin ming*, the *Song of Enlightenment* provides guidance to all Seon practitioners. In Korea, the printing woodblocks for this work carved in the 26th year of the Goryeo King Gojong's reign (September 1239) under the title *Nammyeongcheon hwasangsong jeungdoga* (南明泉和尙頌證道歌; *Song of Enlightenment Recited by Ven. Nan Mingquan*) are still preserved. These printing blocks have been designated as Korean Treasure No. 758 and are housed in the Samseong Museum of Publishing.

Following is an excerpt from the *Song of Enlightenment*.

> Have you not seen the leisurely ones
> Who have gone beyond learning and abide in the Way?
> They neither expunge false thoughts nor seek after the truth.
> Ignorance is intrinsically the Buddha nature,
> And our illusory, empty body is the body of the Dharma.
> When we awaken to the Dharma body, there is nothing at all.
> The source of our self-nature is the Buddha of innocent truth.

🢂 증도가(證道歌)

《증도가》는 깨달음을 증득한 게송을 담은 선어록이다. '증(證)'이란 깨친 자리이고, '도(道)'란 만인이 모두 똑같이 이행해야 하는 도리이며, '가(歌)'란 운치 있게 소리와 리듬을 조율한 시다. 당나라 영가현각(665~713) 선사가 육조혜능 선사를 만나 하루 만에 깨달음을 인가받고 지었다고 한다. 대오의 심경을 266구 1,814자의 고시체로 읊은 시로서 8세기 초에 저술된 것으로 추정된다.

《신심명》과 더불어 선가의 대표적인 명저로 수많은 세월 동안 모든 선객의 나침반이 되었다. 우리나라에는 고려 고종 26년(1239년 9월) 목판본으로 번각한 《남명천화상송증도가(南明泉和尙頌證道歌)》(보물 758호, 삼성출판박물관 소장)가 있다.

아래는 《증도가》의 일부분이다.

       그대는 보지 못하였는가.
       배움이 끊어진 일 없는 한가한 도인은
       망상도 없애지 않고 참됨도 구하지 않으니
       무명의 참 성품이 바로 불성이요
       허깨비 같은 빈 몸이 곧 법신이로다.
       법신을 깨달음에 한 물건도 없으니
       근원의 자성이 천진불이라
       君不見
       絶學無爲閑道人 不除妄想不求眞
       無明實性卽佛性 幻化空身卽法身
       法身覺了無一物 本源自性天眞佛

Fill in the Blanks

❖ 1. "Jeung (증)" refers to the enlightened _____. (상태)

❖ 2. "Do (도)" refers to the _____ all people must put into practice. (진리)

❖ 3. "Ga (가)" refers to a poem in which sound and _____ are gracefully harmonized (리듬)

❖ 4. On the day after his enlightenment was _____ by the Sixth Patriarch Huineng (확인하다, 인증하다)

❖ 5. It is written in the style of old Chinese _____. (시)

❖ 6. As one of the _____ of the Seon School (명저, 걸작)

❖ 7. The *Song of Enlightenment* provides _____ to all Seon practitioners. (지침)

❖ 8. In Korea, the printing _____ for this work are still preserved. (목판)

❖ 9. These woodblocks were _____ in the 26th year of the Goryeo King Gojong's reign (September 1239). (새기다)

❖ 10. These printing blocks have been _____ Korean Treasure No. 758. (지정되다)

❖ 11. They are housed in the Samseong Museum of _____. (출판)

❖ 12. Following is an _____ from the *Song of Enlightenment*. (발췌)

Questions

1. What does the *Song of Enlightenment* describe?
2. Who composed the *Song of Enlightenment*?
3. Who certified the enlightenment of Seon Master Yongjia Xuanjue?
4. Does the *Song of Enlightenment* function as a guide to all Korean Seon practitioners?
5. Was the *Song of Enlightenment* carved onto printing woodblocks during the Goryeo era?

Unit 5

The *Mirror of Seon* (禪家龜鑑; *Seonga gwigam*)

Seonga gwigam was authored by Great Master Seosan Hyujeong (西山休靜; 1520~1604). It is a guide to Seon practice that can be used as a mirror for Seon practitioners. Master Seosan wanted to produce the book because he was greatly disappointed at the way his contemporaries learned Buddhism. After deep reflection, he concluded that disciples of the Buddha regarded only the sacred texts of the Buddhist canon as precious. Then he collected essential passages from Buddhist canons and recorded sayings of Seon masters and organized them. To these he added annotations, commentaries, and verses, producing *Seonga gwigam*. Hence, the book may be used to initiate students into the Seon School.

In addition, the book was written to mediate the confrontation that existed between the Seon and Doctrinal Schools at the time. Master Seosan said, "Seon is the mind of the Buddha while Doctrine is the words of the Buddha (禪是佛心 教是佛語)." By this, he recognized the superiority of Seon over Doctrine, but he also clarified that Seon and Doctrine were not in opposition but actually complemented each other.

In *Seonga gwigam*, there are an introduction written by Master Seosan and an epilogue written by his disciple, Great Master Samyeong Yujeong (四溟 惟政; 1544~1610). The first Chinese edition was published in 1579 and printed from woodblocks. Since then, *Seonga gwigam* has been continuously published, both in Chinese and in Korean, by many temples including Songgwang-sa and Bohyeon-sa. Especially in the late Joseon era, it received much attention from scholars of the practical learning movement called "*silhak* (實學)." In addition, *Seonga gwigam* was popular and frequently published in Japan to such an extent that there were 180 different editions by the late 17th century.

The following are excerpts from the beginning of *Seonga gwigam*.

There is a single thing that from its origin has been ever so bright and ever so numinous, never born and never extinguished, that cannot be named and cannot be described.

The Buddhas and patriarchs appear in the world stirring up waves in the absence of wind.

However, the Dharma has many meanings, and people have many capacities; it is permissible to employ skillful means accordingly.

▶ 선가귀감(禪家龜鑑)

《선가귀감》은 서산대사(1520~1604) 휴정스님이 지은 책으로 말 그대로 선가에서 거울로 삼을 수 있는 지침서이다. 서산대사가 이 책을 저술한 것은 당시 불교를 배우는 사람들의 행태를 보고 크게 실망하였기 때문이다. 숙고 끝에 '불제자들이 보배로 여긴 것은 오로지 대장경의 거룩한 글 뿐'이라는 결론을 내리고, 대장경과 선사의 어록 가운데서 요긴한 것을 추려 모아 정리하였다. 그리고 거기에 손수 주석을 달고 평과 송을 덧붙여서 《선가귀감》을 만들었다. 따라서 이 책은 선종 입문서적인 성격을 갖는다.

또한 선종과 교종으로 대립하던 당시의 불교 상황을 타개하기 위해 저술한 종합개론서이기도 하다. 서산대사는 "선은 곧 부처의 마음이고 교는 곧 부처의 말씀(禪是佛心 教是佛語)"이라 했다. 즉 선의 교에 대한 우월성을 인정하긴 했으나 선과 교는 상호대립적인 관계가 아니라 서로 보완될 수 있음을 밝혔다.

본서의 내용에는 저자 서산대사의 서문과 그 제자인 사명대사의 발문이 함께 있다. 초판은 1579년 원문인 한문본으로 판각되었다. 《선가귀감》은 송광사, 보현사 등 여러 사찰에서 한문본 뿐만 아니라 언해본으로도 꾸준히 간행되어 왔고, 특히 조선 후기에 이르러 실학자들에 의해 주목받았다. 또한 일본에서도 자주 간행되었는데 17세기 이후에는 180여 종에 이르는 간행본이 있을 정도로 유행하였다. 다음은 《선가귀감》의 초입부이다.

하나의 그 무엇이 여기에 있다. 그것은 본래부터 밝디 밝으며 신령스럽고 신령스럽지만 생성한 적도 없고 소멸한 적도 없으니 이름을 붙일 수도 없고 형상을 그려 나타낼 수도 없다.
有一物於此, 從本以來, 昭昭靈靈, 不曾生, 不曾滅, 名不得, 狀不得.

부처님과 조사가 세상에 나온 것은 바람도 불지 않는 곳에서 물결을 일으킨 것과 같다.
佛祖出世, 無風起浪.

그러나 법에는 다양한 뜻이 있고 사람에게는 수많은 근기가 있으니, 그에 따르는 방편을 세워도 무방하다.
然, 法有多義, 人有多機, 不妨施設.

Fill in the Blanks

- 1. *Seonga gwigam* was _____ by Great Master Seosan Hyujeng. (저술하다)
- 2. It is a guide to Seon practice that can be used as a _____ for Seon practitioners. (귀감)
- 3. Master Seosan was greatly disappointed at the way his _____ learned Buddhism. (동시대인)
- 4. After _____ _____, he concluded that disciples of the Buddha regarded only the sacred texts of the Buddhist canon as precious. (숙고)
- 5. To these he added _____, commentaries, and verses, producing *Seonga gwigam*. (주석)
- 6. Hence, the book may be used to _____ students into the Seon School. (입문시키다)
- 7. In addition, the book was written to _____ the confrontation that existed between the Seon and Doctrinal Schools at the time. (중재하다)
- 8. Seon is the _____ of the Buddha while Doctrine is the words of the Buddha. (마음)
- 9. By this, he recognized the _____ of Seon over Doctrine. (우월성)
- 10. He also clarified that Seon and Doctrine were not in opposition but actually _____ each other. (보완하다)
- 11. The first _____ _____ was published in 1579 and printed from woodblocks. (한문본)
- 12. Especially in the late Joseon era, it received much attention from scholars of the _____ learning movement called "Silhak." (현실적인, 실용적인)

Questions

1. Why did Master Seosan want to write *Seonga gwigam*?
2. Did Seosan include essential passages from recorded sayings of Seon masters?
3. Was it part of the purpose of *Seonga gwisgam* to resolve the confrontation between the Seon and Doctrinal Schools?
4. When was the first edition of *Seonga gwigam* published?
5. Was *Seonga gwigam* popular in Japan?

Chapter 3

Seon Practice in Korea
한국의 선수행

Unit 1 — Instructions for Sitting Seon (坐禪儀; *Zuochanyi*)

Zuochanyi (坐禪儀; Kr. *Jwaseonu*i) is a classic beginner's book for seated Seon meditation which explains how to practice Seon. The author, Cijue Zongze (慈覺宗賾: 1009~1092), was a monk of the Yunmen House in the Song Dynasty. From 1102 to 1105, Cijue Zongze served as the abbot of the Hongji Seon Center (洪濟禪院) in Hebei Province where he compiled the 10 volumes of *Pure Rules for Seon Temples* (禪院清規; *Chanyuan qinggui*). He authored the book in order to "revive the old tradition of the *Pure Rules of Baizhang* (百丈清規)." The eighth volume of this 10-volume set is *Zuochanyi*.

In 1233 in Japan, after more than 100 years since *Zuochanyi* had been printed in China, Dogen (道元; 1200~1253) published *Universally Recommended Instructions* for *Zazen* (普勸坐禪儀; Jp. *Fukan zazengi*). Dogen mentioned that he wrote the book based on the *Zuochanyi*, which was part of the *Chanyuan qinggui*.

In Korea, Ven. Beopjeong first translated the *Zuochanyi* into Korean and published it as part of a training text when he served as the director of the Buddhist training center at Songgwang-sa Temple in 1980s. Thus, the Korean translation, titled *Jwaseonui* (坐禪儀), was first introduced to the Korean public after more than 870 years since it had been first published in China.

Cijue Zongze's *Zuochanyi* lists 10 principles of Sitting Seon as follows: 1) Making a great vow (誓願), 2) Giving up worldly involvement (捨緣), 3) Regulating one's diet (調食), 4) Regulating one's sleep so that one does not sleep neither too much nor too little (調眠), 5) Selecting one's place of practice (擇處),

6) Harmonizing one's body (調身), 7) Calming one's breathing (調息), 8) Taming one's thoughts (調心), 9) Understanding harmful obstructions to one's practice (辨魔), 10) Protecting and maintaining one's practice (護持). Following is an excerpt from the *Zuochanyi*.

> The Bodhisattva who studies prajñā
> Should first arouse a thought of great compassion,
> Make the great vows, and then carefully cultivate samādhi.
> Vowing to save sentient beings,
> He should not seek liberation for himself alone;
> Then cast aside all worldly involvement and discontinue all worldly affairs;
> Make body and mind one, with no division between movement and stillness;
> Regulate food and drink, taking neither too much nor too little;
> Adjust sleep, neither be deprived nor indulged.

좌선의(坐禪儀)

〈좌선의〉는 좌선하는 방법을 설명한 고전적인 좌선 입문서이다. 저자 자각종색(慈覺宗賾: 1009~1092)은 중국 송나라 때 운문종에 속한 스님이다. 1102~1105년경 자각종색스님은 하북성 홍제선원의 주지로 있으면서 선종 사원의 독자적인 계율인《선원청규(禪院淸規)》10권을 저술하였다. 스님이 '옛 백장청규(百丈淸規)의 전통을 되살리고자' 편찬한 이 10권의 저서 중 제 8권이 〈좌선의〉다.

일본에서는 중국보다 100여 년이 지난 1233년에 도겐(道元)스님의 〈보권좌선의(普勸坐禪儀)〉가 나왔다. 도겐스님은 백장의《선원청규》에 실린 〈좌선의〉를 근거로 이 책을 썼다고 밝히고 있다.

우리나라에서는 1980년대 송광사 수련원 장이었던 법정스님이 수련 교재에 자각종색스님의 〈좌선의〉를 번역하여 실은 것이 효시가 되어 일반에게 널리 알려지게 되었다. 〈좌선의〉가 나온 지 870여 년만의 일이다.

자각종색 선사의 〈좌선의〉에서는 좌선의 기본법칙으로 열 가지를 제시하고 있다. 첫째는 큰 원을 발하는 것(誓願), 둘째는 모든 인연을 놓는 것(捨緣), 셋째는 음식을 조절하는 것(調食), 넷째는 잠을 조절하는 것(調眠), 다섯째는 처소를 선택하는 것(擇處), 여섯째는 몸을 조정하는 것(調身), 일곱째는 호흡을 고르는 것(調息), 여덟째는 마음을 고르는 것(調心), 아홉째는 마장을 판단하는 것(辨魔), 열째는 두호하여 지켜나가는 것(護持)이다. 다음은 〈좌선의〉의 일부분이다.

반야(般若)를 배우는 보살은

먼저 대비심(大悲心)을 일으키고,

큰 서원을 발하여,

정밀하게 삼매(三昧)를 닦아서,

중생을 제도해야 되겠다는 서원을 세울 것이요,

자신만을 위하여 홀로 해탈을 구하지 말아야 한다.

모든 반연을 놓아버리고 모든 일을 쉬어서,

몸과 마음이 한결 같고 움직이고 고요함에 틈이 없어야 한다.

음식을 헤아려서 많이 먹거나 적게 먹지 말고,

수면을 조절해서 부족하거나 지나치지 않게 해야 한다.

Fill in the Blanks

❖ 1. *Zuochanyi* (좌선의; Kr. *Jwaseonui*) is a classic _____ _____ for seated Seon Meditation. (입문서)

❖ 2. The author was a monk of the _____ _____ in the Song Dynasty. (운문종)

❖ 3. From 1102 to 1105, Cijue Zongze served as the _____ of the Hongji Seon Center (흥제선원) in Hebei Province. (주지)

❖ 4. He authored the book in order to "_____ the old tradition of the Pure Rules of Baizhang (백장청규)." (되살리다)

❖ 5. The eighth _____ of this 10-volume set is *Zuochanyi*. (권)

❖ 6. In Korea, Ven. Beopjeong first translated the *Zuochanyi* into Korean and published it as part of a _____ _____. (수련서)

❖ 7. Cijue Zongze's *Zuochanyi* lists 10 _____ of Sitting Seon.

❖ 8. The Bodhisattva who studies prajna should first _____ a thought of great compassion. (일으키다)

❖ 9. Make the great vows, and then carefully _____ samādhi. (닦다)

❖ 10. Vowing to save sentient beings, he should not seek _____ for himself alone. (해탈)

❖ 11. Then cast aside all _____ _____. (세속적 관여, 반연)

- 12. Make body and mind one, with no division between movement and _____. (정)
- 13. _____ food and drink, taking neither too much nor too little. (조절하다)
- 14. Adjust sleep, neither be _____ nor indulged. (결핍된)

Questions

1. What does *Zuochanyi* explain?
2. Which sect of Buddhism did Cijue Zongze belong to?
3. Where did Cijue Zongze write the *Pure Rules for Seon Temples* (禪院清規)?
4. Is *Zuochanyi* (坐禪儀) a part of the *Pure Rules for Seon Temples* (禪院清規)?
5. Who first translated *Zuochanyi* into Korean?

Unit 2

Practice of Ganhwa Seon (看話禪) 간화선 수행

2.1 - The Three Essentials of Ganhwa Seon

Master Gaofeng Yuanmiao (高峰原妙 1238~1295) emphasized in his *Gist of Seon* (禪要; *Chanyao*) that a student of the *hwadu* (話頭) must possess three essential qualities of mind: "great faith, great fury, and great doubt." Cultivation of mind can be compared to balancing the three sides of a triangle, and if even one of the three is missing, the triangle cannot exist. The following explains the three essentials for *hwadu* investigation as presented in Gaofeng Yuanmiao's *Chanyao*.

> If you really want to practice, you should cultivate these three essential qualities.
> First, you must have great faith (大信心), as unwavering as though you were relying on Mt. Sumeru.
> Secondly, you must have great fury (大憤志), as fierce as though you just met the bitter enemy who killed your parents and you were about to slash him in half.
> Thirdly, you must have great doubt (大疑情), as strong as when you have just finished an important matter in complete darkness, want to reveal it soon, but have not revealed it yet.
> If you cultivate these three essential qualities, you can surely make progress before even a single day has passed. This is as certain as a terrapin kept in a pot not escaping from it. However, if even one quality is missing, your practice will be as useless as a two-legged tripod.

간화선의 세 가지 중요한 요점

고봉원묘 선사는 《선요》에서 화두 공부인은 대신심(大信心), 대분심(大憤心), 대의심(大疑心)의 세 가지 요소를 갖춰야 한다고 강조했다. 마음공부는 삼각형의 세 변과 같아서 하나라도 없으면 삼각형은 이루어지지 못하는 것과 같은 원리이다. 다음은 고봉선사의 《선요》에 나타난 간화 삼요에 대한 법문이다.

만약 진실로 참선하고자 한다면 반드시 세 가지 중요한 요소를 갖추어야 한다.
첫째, 크게 믿는 마음[大信根]이 있어야 하니, 이 일은 수미산을 의지한 것과 같이 흔들림이 없어야 함을 알아야 한다.
둘째, 크게 분한 생각[大憤志]이 있어야 하니, 마치 부모를 죽인 원수를 만났을 때 그 원수를 당장 한 칼에 두 동강을 내려는 것과 같다.
셋째, 커다란 의심[大疑情]이 있어야 되니, 마치 어두운 곳에서 한 가지 중요한 일을 하고 곧 드러내고자 하나 드러나지 않은 때와 같이 하는 것이다.
온종일 이 세 가지 요소를 갖출 수 있다면 반드시 하루가 다하기 전에 공을 이루는 것이 독 속에 있는 자라가 달아날까 두려워하지 않겠지만, 만일 이 가운데 하나라도 빠지면 마치 다리 부러진 솥이 마침내 못 쓰는 그릇이 되는 것과 같다.

Fill in the Blanks

❖ 1. Master Gaofeng Yuanmiao _____ in his *Gist of Seon* that a student of the *hwadu* must possess three essential qualities of mind. (강조하다)

❖ 2. Cultivation of mind can be compared to balancing the three sides of a _____. (삼각형)

❖ 3. If you really want to _____, you should cultivate these three essential qualities. (수행하다)

❖ 4. First, you must have great faith (대신심), as _____ as though you were relying on Mt. Sumeru. (흔들림 없는)

❖ 5. Secondly, you must have great _____ (대분지), as fierce as though you just met the bitter enemy who killed your parents. (분심)

❖ 6. Thirdly, you must have great _____ (대의정). (의심)

❖ 7. As when you have just finished an important matter in complete darkness, want to _____ it soon, but have not revealed it yet. (드러내다)

❖ 8. If you cultivate these three essential qualities, you can surely make progress before even a _____ _____ has passed. (하루)

❖ 9. This is as certain as a _____ kept in a pot not escaping from it. (자라)

❖ 10. However, if even one quality is missing, your practice will be as _____ as a two-legged tripod. (쓸모없는)

Questions

1. Who said that Seon practitioners should have three essential qualities of mind?
2. What are these three essential qualities of mind?
3. What did Master Gaofeng compare the unwavering quality of great faith to?
4. What did Master Gaofeng compare the fierce quality of great fury to?
5. What happens if one of the three essential qualities of mind is missing?

Unit 2

2.2 - *Hwadu* (話頭) and *Gongan* (公案)

Seon meditation's goal is to break through the barriers set up by the patriarchs. In Seon practice, one can become a patriarch, free from life and death, after one has broken through the completely closed, gateless barrier called the "*hwadu*." Patriarchs use *hwadu*s as their own distinctive language to block all passages of thought and discrimination for practitioners. This language cannot be understood by ordinary thinking. A *hwadu* has the power to sever all discriminating thoughts on the mundane level. That's why *hwadu*s are sometimes called "extraordinary words."

To such questions as "Why did Bodhidharma come from the West?" or "What is the truth?" answers like "The cypress tree in the courtyard" or "A dry shit stick" are extraordinary words on an absolute dimension that transcends the relative dimensions. These words contain inherent truth which is not approachable by words or thought. One can attain enlightenment upon just hearing those *hwadu*s.

A *hwadu* is also called a *gongan* (公案; public case) or a *gochik* (古則). The word "*gongan*" originally meant "official government documents." In other words, it refers to absolute regulations to be observed which also provide standards.

*Gongan*s record the sayings, activities, and enlightened views of Seon masters. It is often said that there are as many as 1,700 *gongan*s. They come from the opportune conditions and behaviors of the 1,701 Seon masters who appear in the *Record of the Transmission of the Lamp* (傳燈錄; *Chuandeng lu*). However, in reality, only 1,650 *gongan*s are found in major collections of *gongan* such as: *The Gateless Barrier* (無門關; *Wumen guan*), the *Blue Cliff Record* (碧巖錄; *Biyanlu*), and *Compilation of Examinations of and Verses on Ancient Precedents* (禪門拈頌; *Seonmun yeomsong*).

화두(話頭), 공안(公案)

참선이란 조사의 관문을 뚫는 것이다. 선에서는 화두라는 꽉 닫힌 문 없는 관문을 뚫고 나간 뒤라야 생사를 벗어나 조사가 될 수 있다. 화두란 모든 사유와 분별의 통로를 막는 선사들의 독특한 언어이다. 그리고 이러한 말은 일상적인 생각으로는 파악될 수 없다. 화두는 상식적으로 생각하는 사유분별을 끊어버리는 힘이 있다. 그래서 화두를 일상적인 격을 벗어났다 하여 격외어(格外語)라 한다.

"무엇이 조사가 서쪽에서 온 뜻이냐?", "무엇이 진리냐?"라는 물음에 "뜰 앞의 잣나무다", "마른 똥 막대기다"라고 대답하는 격외어는 상대적인 말을 초월한 절대적인 말이다. 이것은 말길이 끊어지고 생각의 길도 끊어진 진짜 말이다. 이러한 화두를 바로 깨달으면 된다.

화두를 공안 또는 고칙(古則)이라고도 한다. 공안은 원래 '관청의 공문서'라는 뜻에서 유래한 것이다. 곧 표준이면서 준수해야 하는 절대적인 규범을 의미한다.

이렇듯 공안은 옛 선사들의 언행과 깨달음의 기록이다. 공안은 매우 많아 보통 1,700 공안이라 한다. 이는 《전등록》에 등장하는 1,701분의 선사들이 보여준 기연과 언행에서 유래한 것이다. 그러나 대표적인 공안집이라 할 수 있는 《무문관》·《벽암록》·《선문염송》 등을 보면 실제로 1,650여 가지의 공안이 나와 있다.

Fill in the Blanks

❖ 1. Seon meditation's goal is to break through the _____ set up by the patriarchs. (관문)

❖ 2. In Seon practice, one can become a patriarch, _____ _____ life and death, after one has broken through the "*hwadu*." (벗어나)

❖ 3. Patriarchs use *hwadu*s as their own distinctive language to _____ all thought and discrimination by practitioners. (막다)

❖ 4. This language cannot be understood by _____ thinking. (상식적, 평범한)

❖ 5. A *hwadu* has the power to _____ all discriminating thoughts on the mundane level. (끊다)

❖ 6. That's why *hwadu*s are sometimes called "_____ words." (격외의, 상식을 벗어난)

❖ 7. Why did Bodhidharma come from the _____? (서쪽)

❖ 8. The cypress tree in the _____. (뜰, 마당)

❖ 9. A dry shit _____ (막대기)

❖ 10. These words contain inherent truth which is not _____ by words or thought. (접근할 수 있는)

❖ 11. The word "*gongan*" originally meant "official government _____." (문서)

❖ 12. *Gongan* refers to _____ regulations to be observed which also provide standards. (절대적)

❖ 13. *Gongan*s come from the _____ _____ and behaviors of the 1,701 Seon masters. (기연)

❖ 14. However, in reality, only 1,650 *gongan*s are found in _____ collections of *gongan*. (주요)

❖ 15. *The Blue _____ Record* (벽암록; *Biyanlu*)

Questions

1. Is a *hwadu* a kind of gateless barrier set up by patriarchs?
2. Why do patriarchs use *hwadu*s?
3. Can a *hwadu* be understood by ordinary thinking?
4. Where did the word *gongan* originate?
5. How many *gongan*s are there?

2.3 - Implementation of *Manhaeng* (萬行) and Seon Practice

After finishing the three-month Seon meditation retreat, most Seon practitioners enter into traveling practices called "*manhaeng*," also called "*haenggak* (行脚)." This is the time when practitioners test themselves to see if they can practice *hwadu* well or if their minds are unwavering even in the midst of various earthly situations. During *manhaeng*, the emphasis is not on wandering itself but on visiting other places of learning. That's why virtuous masters say, "The end of a retreat is the beginning of another." Therefore, during *manhaeng*, practitioners should keep in mind that there is no place where learning can not occur, and they must never cease their *hwadu* practice. Traveling practice exists for the sake of practice.

Pertaining to this, Seon Master Wuzu Fayan (五祖法演; 1024~1104) gave the following advice to a practitioner who was about to leave on traveling practice. It is from his *Dongshan chongzangzhu songzi xingjiao fayu* (東山崇藏主送子行脚法語).

> In general, you must always be with the Way during traveling practice. You must not idle time away just eating the food you are offered. Keep the two words "life" and "death" in the center of your forehead and contemplate thoroughly the *hwadu* of "life and death." Do this all day long until you find the answer. If you idle your time away hanging around with mindless companions, then the King of Hell, Yama, will make you repay the cost of every meal you ever ate at the time of your death. At that time, do not complain that I did not forewarn you.

▶▶ 만행(萬行)의 실천과 선수행

보통 선원에서 참선하는 납자들은 세 달 동안 안거를 끝낸 뒤에 만행에 들어간다. 만행이란 행각(行脚)이라고도 하는데 갖가지 세상 경계 속에서 화두가 제대로 들리는지, 자신의 마음이 흔들리지 않는지를 점검해 보는 진지한 자기 시험이기도 하다. 행각은 행각 자체에 목적이 있는 것이 아니라 또 다른 공부처를 찾아가는 것이다. 그래서 선지식들은 해제가 곧 결제라고 했다. 그러므로 공부처가 곳곳에 있다는 사실을 명심하여 만행 중이라도 절대 화두 공부를 놓아서는 안 된다. 만행도 공부를 위해서 있는 것이기 때문이다.

이와 관련하여 오조법연 선사는 《동산숭장주송자행각법어(東山崇藏主送子行脚法語)》에서 행각을 떠나는 공부인에게 다음과 같이 말하고 있다.

> 무릇 행각을 할 때에는 도를 품고 해야 한다. 주는 공양을 먹으면서 한가하게 세월을 보내지 말아야 한다. 모름지기 생사(生死)의 두 글자를 이마 가운데 두고 하루 내내 철저하게 생사의 화두를 생각하고 또 생각해 이를 분명히 찾아내야 한다. 만약 무리를 따르고 떼를 쫓아서 헛되이 세월을 보낸다면 죽을 때에 염라대왕이 밥값을 청구할 것이다. 그때 내가 너를 위해 설해 주지 않았다고 이르지 말지니라.

Fill in the Blanks

❖ 1. After finishing the three-month Seon meditation retreat, most Seon practitioners enter into _____ practices called "*manhaeng*." (여행하는)

❖ 2. This is the time when practitioners test themselves to see if they can practice *hwadu* well even in the midst of various _____ _____. (세상 경계)

❖ 3. During *manhaeng*, the emphasis is not on wandering itself but on visiting other places of _____. (공부)

❖ 4. That's why _____ _____ say, "The end of a retreat is the beginning of another." (선지식)

❖ 5. Therefore, during *manhaeng*, practitioners should _____ ___ _____ that there is no place where learning cannot occur. (명심하다)

❖ 6. _____ _____ this, Seon Master Wuzu Fayan gave the following advice to a practitioner who was about to leave on traveling practice. (관련하여)

❖ 7. In general, you must always ____ _____ the Way during traveling practice. (함께하다)

❖ 8. You must not _____ time _____ just eating the food you are offered. (허비하다)

❖ 9. Keep the two words "life" and "death" in the center of your _____. (이마)

❖ 10. _____ thoroughly the *hwadu* of "life and death." (생각하다)

❖ 11. The King of Hell, Yama, will make you _____ the cost of every meal you ever ate at the time of your death. (갚다)

❖ 12. At that time, do not complain that I did not _____ you. (미리 알려주다)

Questions

1. What does *manhaeng* refer to?
2. What do practitioners do during *manhaeng*?
3. Do practitioners investigate *hwadu* during their *manhaeng* practice?
4. What should *manhaeng* practitioners keep in mind?
5. In *manhaeng* practice, is the emphasis on wandering itself?

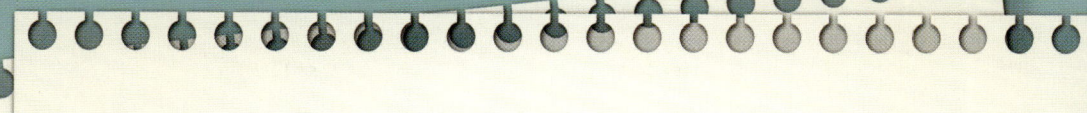

쉬어가는 코너

The one, who while young devotes himself
To the Teaching of the Buddha,
Illuminates this world like the moon
Freed from clouds.

– Theragatha

젊은 시절 부처님의 가르침을
열심히 배우고 닦은 사람은
구름을 벗어난 달처럼
세상을 환히 비춘다

– 장로게

Part 3

Ceremonies of Korean Buddhism

한국불교의 의례

- Chapter 1 **Temple Ceremonies** 사찰의례

- Chapter 2 **Cheondo-jae** 천도재

- Chapter 2 **Eminent Monks of Korea** 한국의 고승

Chapter 1

Temple Ceremonies

사찰 의례

Unit 1 — The Dawn Bell Chant

The "dawn bell chant" is performed while sounding the bell at the early morning Buddhist ceremony. The dawn bell chant starts upon the end of *Doryangseok* (道場釋), a chanting ceremony to purify and awaken the temple compound. The dawn bell chant saves sentient beings from the suffering of hell and guides them to be reborn in the Pure Land. Listening to the chant (鍾頌), sentient beings awaken to the spiritual power of Amitabha Buddha and the splendor of the Pure Land and then take refuge in the Buddhas and bodhisattvas. In terms of rhythm and tune, bell chants are a type of *beompae* (梵唄), verses sung in praise of the Buddha and his teachings. Thus, bell chants are deemed important as they have characteristics of Korean traditional music.

> May the sound of this bell spread throughout the universe,
> Lift the thick darkness over the Great Iron Mountains,
> Relieve the three realms of suffering and shatter the hell of swords,
> And bring all sentient beings to perfect enlightenment.

새벽종송

아침 예불을 올릴 때 종을 치며 하는 새벽종송은 도량석이 끝나면서 시작된다. 전체적인 의미는 아미타불의 위신력과 극락세계의 장엄을 설하여 지옥의 고통 받는 중생들이 종송을 듣고서 불보살님께 귀의하여 왕생극락하도록 구제하는데 있다. 종송의 음률은 범패의 일종으로 한국 전통음악의 특수한 선율을 지니고 있어 중요시된다.

이 종소리 온 법계에 두루 퍼져	願此鐘聲遍法界
철위산 깊은 어둠 다 걷히고	鐵圍幽暗悉皆明
삼도 고통 없어지고 칼산지옥 무너져서	三途離苦破刀山
일체중생 바른 깨침 이뤄지이다.	一切衆生成正覺

Fill in the Blanks

❖ 1. The "dawn bell chant" is performed while _____ the bell at the early morning Buddhist ceremony. (울리다)

❖ 2. The dawn bell chant starts _____ the end of *Doryangseok*. (~하자마자)

❖ 3. It is a chanting ceremony to _____ and awaken the temple compound. (청정하게 하다)

❖ 4. The dawn bell chant saves sentient beings from the suffering of hell and guides them to be _____ in the Pure Land. (왕생하다)

❖ 5. Listening to the chant, sentient beings awaken to the _____ power of Amitabha Buddha and the _____ of the Pure Land. (영적, 장엄)

❖ 6. In terms of rhythm and tune, bell chants are a type of *beompae* (범패), verses sung in _____ of the Buddha and his teachings. (찬탄)

❖ 7. Thus, bell chants are deemed important as they have characteristics of Korean _____ _____. (전통음악)

❖ 8. May the sound of this bell _____ throughout the universe (퍼지다)

❖ 9. Lift the thick _____ over the Great Iron Mountains (어둠)

❖ 10. Relieve the three realms _____ suffering. (으로부터)

❖ 11. And _____ the hell of swords (무너뜨리다)

❖ 12. And bring all sentient beings to perfect _____. (깨달음)

Questions

1. What ceremony is the dawn bell chant a part of?
2. Is the dawn bell chant accompanied by sounding the temple bell?
3. After what ritual does the dawn bell chant start?
4. Why is the bell chant regarded a type of *beompae*?
5. Are Buddhist bell chants deemed important by the Korean music community?

Unit 2

Yebul, Morning and Evening Buddhist Ceremonies

The Buddhist ceremony called *yebul* is offered to pay homage to all Buddhas and bodhisattvas. *Yebul* is also practiced to cultivate oneself. Buddhists offer these ceremonies twice a day, in the morning and in the evening. *Yebul* begins with the *Verse of Tea* (茶偈) and is followed by the *Verse of Five Scents* (五分香偈), the *Mantra of Incense Offering* (獻香眞言), and the *Ritual of Seven Prostrations* (七頂禮).

The Verse of Tea

We now offer this pure water as nectar-like tea
To the Buddha, the Dharma, and the Sangha.
May this be received in compassion!
May this be received in compassion!
May this be received in great compassion!

The Verse of Five Scents

The sweet scent of our observance of the precepts,
Of our meditative concentration, of our wisdom,
Of our liberation, and of the knowledge of our liberation!
We present these offerings to the countless Buddhas,
Dharma, and Sanghas in all of the ten directions,
In the universe pervaded by brightly lit clouds.

The Mantra of Incense Offering

Om Ba A Ra Do Bi Ya Hum (three times)

The Ritual of Seven Prostrations

With utmost sincerity,
We pay homage to Sakyamuni Buddha,
The teacher of the universe, the loving father of all beings.

With utmost sincerity,
We pay homage to all sacred Buddhas,
Always present in all corners of the universe.

With utmost sincerity,
We pay homage to all the teachings,
Eternally existing in the universe.

With utmost sincerity,
We pay homage to Manjusri, Bodhisattva of great wisdom;
Samantabhadra, Bodhisattva of great action;
Avalokitesvara, Bodhisattva of great compassion;
And Ksitigarbha, Bodhisattva of great vows.

With utmost sincerity,
We pay homage to the ten major disciples, the sixteen holy ones,
The five hundred holy ones, self-enlightened ones,
And all of the one thousand two hundred great arhats,
To whom the Buddha entrusted
The transmission of the teachings.

With utmost sincerity,
We pay homage to those great patriarchs, eminent monks, and countless teachers,
Who have transmitted the lamp of the Dharma over generations.

With utmost sincerity,
We pay homage to all of the sanghas,
Eternally existing in all the ten directions.

The inexhaustible Three Jewels!
We earnestly wish that you receive our devotion,
And bestow your blessings on us.
We further wish that all beings in the universe attain Buddhahood.

🡲 예불

예불은 불보살에 대한 예경의 의미를 지닌 것이며, 자신을 위한 수행의 의미도 함께 지닌 수행이다. 불자들은 하루에 두 차례씩 조석 예불을 올린다.
예불은 다게, 오분향게, 헌향진언, 칠정례의 순으로 행한다.

다게
저희 이제 청정수를 감로다 삼아
삼보님 전 올리오니
자비로 받으소서.
자비로 받으소서.
대자비로 받으옵소서.

오분향게
계향 정향 혜향 해탈향 해탈지견향
광명구름 두루하여 시방세계 한량없는
삼보님전 공양합니다.

헌향진언
옴 바아라 도비야 훔 (3번)

칠정례
지극한 마음으로
온 세계 스승이며 모든 중생 어버이신
석가모니 부처님께 절하옵니다.

지극한 마음으로
온 세계 항상 계신 거룩하신 부처님께 절하옵니다.

지극한 마음으로
온 세계 항상 계신 거룩하신 가르침에 절하옵니다.

지극한 마음으로
대지문수사리보살 대행보현보살
대비관세음보살 대원본존 지장보살님께 절하옵니다.

지극한 마음으로
부처님께 부촉 받은 십대제자 십육성 오백성

독수성 내지 천이백 아라한께 절하옵니다.

지극한 마음으로
불법 전한 역대조사 천하종사 한량없는 선지식께 절하옵니다.

지극한 마음으로
온 세계 항상 계신 거룩하신 스님들께 절하옵니다.

다함없는 삼보시여,
저희 예경 받으시고, 가피력을 내리시어,
법계중생 모두 함께 성불 하여지이다.

Fill in the Blanks

❖ 1. *Yebul* is offered to pay _____ to all Buddhas and bodhisattvas. (예경)

❖ 2. _____ offer *yebul* twice a day, in the morning and evening. (불자들)

❖ 3. *yebul* begins with the _____ *of Tea* (다게)

❖ 4. *Verse of Five* _____ (오분향게)

❖ 5. *the Mantra of* _____ *Offering* (헌향진언)

❖ 6. *Ritual of Seven* _____ (칠정례)

❖ 7. We now offer this pure water as _____ _____ to the Buddha, the Dharma and the Sangha. (감로다)

❖ 8. May this be received in _____! (자비)

❖ 9. The sweet scent of our _____ of the precepts (지킴)

❖ 10. The sweet scent of the _____ of our liberation (해탈지견향)

❖ 11. We present these offerings to the countless Buddhas, Dharma, and Sanghas in all of the _____ _____. (시방)

❖ 12. With _____ _____, we pay homage to Sakyamuni Buddha, the teacher of the universe. (지극한 마음)

❖ 13. We pay homage to all sacred Buddhas, _____ _____ in all corners of the universe. (항상 계신)

❖ 14. Manjusri, Bodhisattva of great _____ (지혜)

❖ 15. Samantabhadra, Bodhisattva of great _____ (행동)

❖ 16. Avalokitesvara, Bodhisattva of great _____ (자비)

❖ 17. And Ksitigarbha, Bodhisattva of great _____ (서원)

❖ 18. We pay homage to the _____ _____ _____, (십대제자)

❖ 19. And all of the one thousand two hundred great arhats, to whom the Buddha _____ the transmission of the teachings. (부촉하다)

❖ 20. We pay homage to those great patriarchs, eminent monks and countless teachers, who have transmitted the _____ of the Dharma over generations. (등불)

❖ 21. The _____ Three Jewels (다함없는)

❖ 22. We earnestly wish that you receive our _____, and bestow your blessings on us. (예경)

Questions

1. Is *yebul* only offered to pay homage to the Buddhas and bodhisattvas?
2. How many times a day do Buddhists offer *yebul*?
3. What ritual does *yebul* begin with?
4. In the *Verse of Five Scents*, what scents are offered?
5. What does the last sentence of *yebul* wish?

Unit 3 — The Evening Bell Chant

The evening bell chant is performed before the evening Buddhist ceremonies. The evening bell chant expresses the hope that all beings expunge all their afflictions, cultivate wisdom, and arouse the Bodhi mind. It further expresses the hope that based on this wisdom and the Bodhi mind, sentient beings will be liberated from hell, attain Buddhahood, and work for the salvation of all other beings.

> Upon hearing the sound of the bell,
> May all beings sever their afflictions, cultivate wisdom,
> Arouse an awakened mind, be delivered from hell,
> Transcend the three realms of samsara,
> Attain enlightenment, and save all people.

▶▶ 저녁종송

저녁종송은 저녁 예불 전에 하는데 그 내용은 일체의 번뇌를 끊고 지혜를 길러 보리심을 냄으로써 지옥을 파하고 삼계를 벗어나 성불하여 모든 중생을 구제하도록 하는 것이다.

이 종소리 듣게 되면 온갖 번뇌 끊어지고	聞鐘聲煩惱斷
청정지혜 자라나며 보리심이 생겨나고	智慧長菩提生
지옥세계 멀리 떠나 삼계를 벗어나고	離地獄出三界
깨달음을 이루어 중생을 건지소서.	願成佛度衆生

Fill in the Blanks

❖ 1. The evening bell chant is performed _____ the evening Buddhist ceremonies. (전에)

❖ 2. The evening bell chant expresses the hope that all beings _____ all their afflictions. (멸하다)

❖ 3. The hope that all beings cultivate wisdom and _____ the Bodhi mind (내다)

❖ 4. It further expresses the hope that sentient beings will be liberated from hell, _____ Buddhahood, and work for the _____ of all sentient beings. (이루다, 구제)

❖ 5. _____ _____ the sound of the bell, may all beings sever their afflictions (들으면)

❖ 6. May all beings cultivate wisdom, arouse an _____ mind (깨달은)

❖ 7. May all beings be _____ from hell, transcend the three realms of samsara (벗어나)

Questions

1. Is the evening bell chant performed before the morning *yebul*?
2. Does the evening bell chant express the hope that all beings sever their afflictions?
3. Does the evening bell chant express the hope that all beings arouse deluded mind?

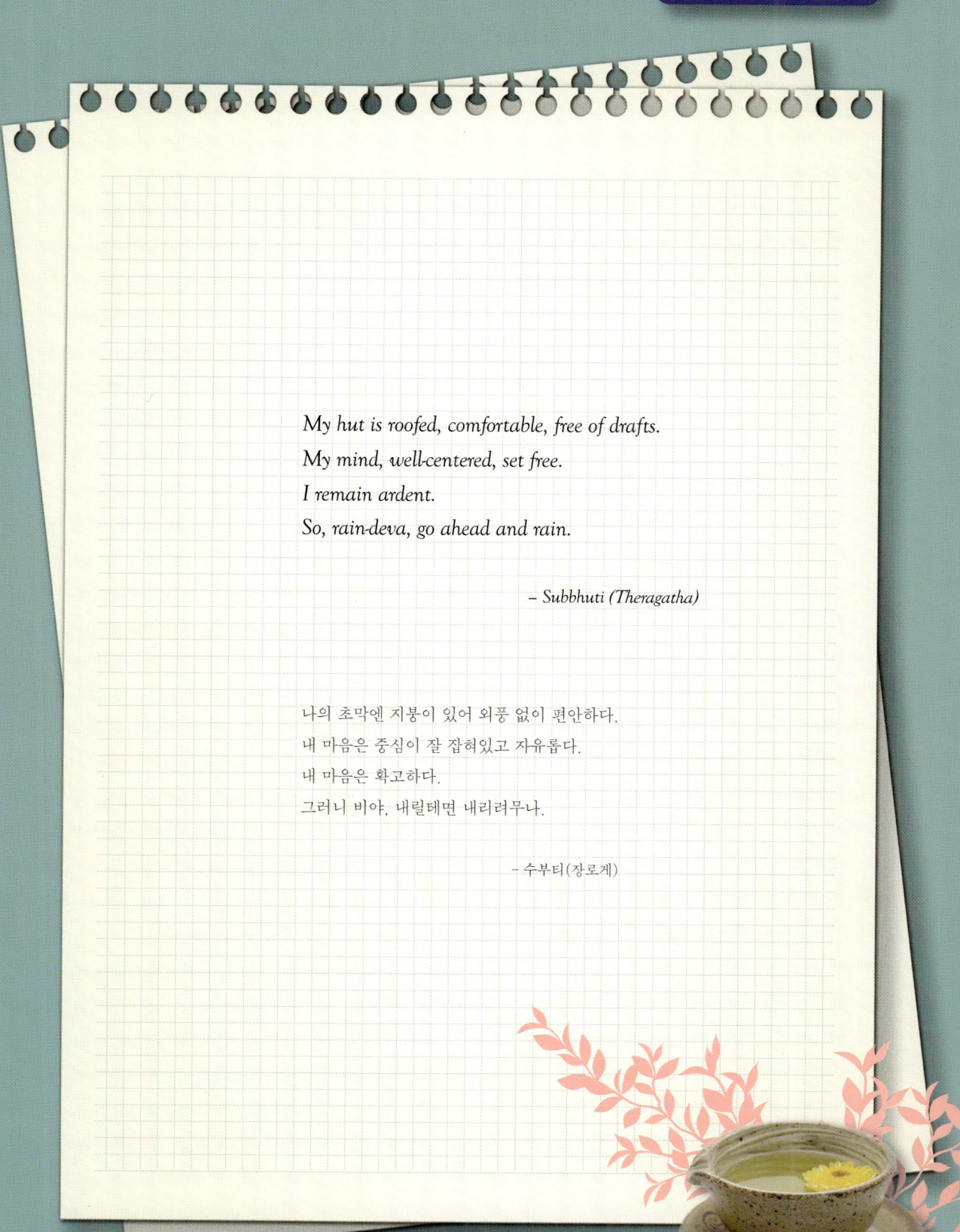

쉬어가는 코너

My hut is roofed, comfortable, free of drafts.
My mind, well-centered, set free.
I remain ardent.
So, rain-deva, go ahead and rain.

— Subbhuti (Theragatha)

나의 초막엔 지붕이 있어 외풍 없이 편안하다.
내 마음은 중심이 잘 잡혀있고 자유롭다.
내 마음은 확고하다.
그러니 비야, 내릴테면 내리려무나.

— 수부티(장로게)

Chapter 2

Cheondo-jae (薦度齋)

천도재(薦度齋)

Cheondo-jae collectively refers to any Buddhist ceremony offered for the deceased. Some of these ceremonies are: *Suryuk-jae* (水陸齋), the ceremony for lonely, wandering spirits in the water and on earth; *Sasipgu-jae* (49齋), the ceremony offered over a period of 49 days from the date of one's death; *Yeongsan-jae* (靈山齋), Korea's traditional dance performance that reenacts the Buddha's teachings at Vulture Peak; and *Yesu-jae* (預修齋), the ceremony in preparation of one's own death. *Cheondo-jae* is intended to expunge all negative karma and resentment that has accumulated during one's life, to purify one's mind, and to help people obtain a favorable rebirth.

Cheondo-jae mostly consists of teachings such as the Formless Precepts (無相戒) so that the spirit of the deceased will understand that death is a natural phenomenon occurring in the flux of all things and thus is nothing to regret. It further exhorts the deceased to be reborn in the Pure Land by arousing in them an aspiration for enlightenment based on the perfect teachings of the Buddha.

천도재란 죽은 사람을 위하여 불교에서 올리는 재례의식들의 총칭으로 수륙재나 49재, 영산재, 예수재 등도 천도재에 속한다. 천도재는 죽은 사람이 생전에 지었던 모든 악업이나 원한 관계 등을 해소하고 청정한 마음을 회복하여 좋은 곳에 태어나도록 돕는다는 의미를 지니고 있다.

천도재의 주된 내용은 영가에게 《무상계》 등을 설하여 죽음이라는 현실은 만물이 변화하는 가운데 도래하는 자연적인 현상으로 크게 안타까워할 일이 아님을 일깨우는 것이다. 더하여 부처님의 바른 가르침에 따라 깨달음을 구하는 마음을 내서 아미타부처님의 극락세계에 왕생할 것을 권하는 설법으로 이루어지고 있다.

Unit 1

Sasipgu-jae (49齋), the Forty-Nine Day Ceremony

"*Sasipgu-jae*" or "Forty-Nine Day Ceremony" is the ceremony offered for the deceased over a period of 49 days, on every seventh day for seven times, as a way to bring peace and eternal rest to those who have died. *Sasipgu-jae* can also be a ritual for the living and for the still living family members of the deceased. For those who struggle with grief and despair after the loss of a family member or friend, a word of truth they hear at this memorial ceremony may serve as the nectar of life.

After the funeral, the family enshrines the spirit tablet and a photo of the deceased at a temple. Every seven days family members and friends gather at the temple and pray that the deceased be reborn in the Pure Land. At this time they often prepare food, fruits, and tea and offer them on the altar for the deceased. This is to console the spirit of the deceased which may have been overwhelmed with loneliness and fear at the intermediate state.

Sasipgu-jae is usually presided over by the most virtuous monks and nuns. The ceremony consists of many steps to offer correct teachings to the deceased including ceremonies for "welcoming the deceased (對靈)" and "bathing the dead (灌浴)." The scriptures and talks presented at the *Sasipgu-jae* ceremony commonly contain the message that the deceased should not be attached to their physical body and illusory reality, which in reality are as insubstantial as bubbles, and find their true self. In addition, the presiding monk guides the deceased to expiate all unwholesome actions by repenting them before Amitabha Buddha and Ksitigarbha Bodhisattva and to pray for a rebirth in the Pure Land.

Listening to all the chanting of scriptures and Dharma talks, the spirit of the deceased calmly looks back at his or her past life and realizes the impermanence of life. Then he or she prepares to depart to a tranquil world where there is no greed, anger, or ignorance. The last step of *Sasipgu-jae* is "sending off the spirit." With this the spirit is guided to the Pure Land where Amitabha Buddha greets him or her.

▶▶ 49재

49재는 사람이 죽은 날로부터 매 칠일 째마다 일곱 차례에 걸쳐 49일 동안 죽은 이의 명복을 기원하는 천도의식이다. 더하여 49재는 남아있는 자들을 위한 의식이기도 하다. 가족이나 친지를 잃어 슬픔과 절망 속에서 허우적거릴 때 49재에서 듣는 진리의 말씀 한마디가 생명의 감로수가 되기도 한다.

망자의 장례가 끝나고 나면 영가(죽은 이)의 위패와 사진을 사찰에 모셔 놓고 매 칠 일마다 가족과 친지들이 모여 영가의 극락왕생을 기원하는 기도와 공양을 올린다. 이때 영가를 위해 제단에 정성껏 마련한 다과와 음식을 차려놓기도 한다. 외로움과 두려움으로 방황하고 있을 영가에 대한 따뜻한 배려의 뜻이다.

49재를 지낼 때는 덕이 높으신 스님이 시방세계에 계신 불보살님을 청하는 대령(對靈), 관욕(灌浴)을 시작으로 여러 단계에 걸쳐 영가에게 바른 가르침을 일러준다. 49재에 독송하는 경전과 법문은 모두 물거품 같은 육신과 허상에 매이지 말고 참된 자기를 깨달으라는 내용을 담고 있다. 더하여 아미타불과 지장보살님에게 모든 죄업을 참회하여 소멸하고 극락왕생을 염원하기도 한다.

이렇게 행해지는 독경과 법문을 듣고 영가는 지난 생을 차분히 되돌아보며 삶의 무상을 깨닫는다. 그리고 탐욕과 성냄과 어리석음이 없는 고요한 세계로 떠날 준비를 한다. 49재의 마지막 봉송 의식을 끝으로 영가는 아미타불의 영접 하에 극락세계로 인도된다.

Fill in the Blanks

❖ 1. *Cheondo-jae* _____ refers to any Buddhist ceremony offered for the deceased. (총괄하여, 집합적으로)

❖ 2. *Suryuk-jae* (수륙재), the ceremony for lonely, _____ spirits in the water and on earth (떠도는)

❖ 3. *Sasipgu-jae* (49재), the ceremony offered over a period of 49 days from the date of one's _____ (죽음)

❖ 4. *Yeongsan-jae* (영산재), Korea's traditional dance performance that _____ the Buddha's teachings at Vulture Peak (재현하다)

❖ 5. *Yesu-jae* (예수재), the ceremony in _____ of one's own death (준비)

❖ 6. *Cheondo-jae* is intended to expunge all negative karma and _____ that accumulate during one's life (원한)

❖ 7. It is offered to help people obtain a _____ _____. (좋은 곳에 태어남)

❖ 8. The spirit of the deceased will understand that death is a natural phenomenon occurring in the _____ of all things. (변화)

❖ 9. "Forty-Nine Day Ceremony" is offered over a period of 49 days, on every _____ _____ seven times (일곱째 날)

❖ 10. *Sasipgu-jae* can also be a _____ for the living and for the still living family members of the deceased. (의례)

❖ 11. After the funeral, the family enshrines the _____ _____ and a photo of the deceased at a temple. (위패)

❖ 12. At this time they often prepare food, fruits, and tea and offer them on the _____ for the deceased. (제단)

❖ 13. This is to console the spirit of the deceased which may have been overwhelmed with loneliness and fear at the _____ state. (중음의)

❖ 14. Including ceremonies for "_____ the dead (관욕)." (씻기다)

❖ 15. The message that the deceased should not be _____ to their physical body and illusory reality (연연하다)

❖ 16. Which in reality are as insubstantial as _____ (물거품)

❖ 17. The _____ monk guides the deceased to expiate all unwholesome actions by repenting them. (집전하는)

❖ 18. The spirit of the deceased calmly _____ _____ _____ his or her past life and realizes the impermanence of life. (뒤돌아보아)

❖ 19. Then he or she prepares to _____ to a tranquil world where there is no greed, anger or ignorance. (떠나다)

❖ 20. The spirit is guided to the Pure Land where Amitabha Buddha _____ him or her. (맞이하다)

Questions

1. Does *Cheondo-jae* consist of only one kind of ceremony?
2. Are all *Cheondo-jae* offered for the deceased?
3. At the *Sasipgu-jae*, is food offered to the deceased?
4. At the *Sasipgu-jae*, what do the participants pray for?
5. What is the last step of *Sasipgu-jae*?

Unit 2

Suryuk-jae (水陸齋), the Water-Land Ceremony

"*Suryuk-jae*" or "Water-Land Ceremony" is a memorial ceremony to placate vengeful spirits wandering on the land or in water and hungry ghosts. The Water-Land Ceremony is said to have begun during the reign of Emperor Wu (武帝) of the Liang Dynasty. Emperor Wu, a devout Buddhist, thought that saving the spirits of the deceased who had no one to offer sacrifices for them, would accrue the foremost merit. He had Ven. Zhigong compile the *Text for the Water-Land Ceremony* (水陸齋儀文) and held a ritual in CE 505 at the Gold Mountain Temple (金山寺) in Jiangsu Province. In Song Dynasty, the *Text for the Water-Land Ceremony* enjoyed renewed popularity and was practiced nationwide.

In Korea, the Water-Land Ceremony was first held in December in the 23rd year of Goryeo King Taejo's reign (940). Later, a hall dedicated to the Water-Land Ceremony was established at Garyang-sa Temple in Suwon in the 21st year of King Gwangjong's reign (970). Ven. Hongu, a disciple of Ven. Iryeon, wrote the *Newly Compiled Text for the Water-Land Ceremony* (新編水陸儀文; *Sinpyeon suryuk uimun*), making the ceremony even more popular. In 1397, King Taejo, who founded the Joseon Dynasty, established a Water-Land Ceremony Building (水陸社) which had a total area of 59 bays. There he held the ceremony to appease the spirits of the Wang clan, the royal family of the former Goryeo Dynasty. Afterward, King Taejo held magnificent state-sponsored ceremonies biannually, on the 15th day of the 2nd and 10th lunar month. Beginning from the 15th year of King Taejong' sreign (1415), the ceremony was offered once a year on the 15th day of the 1st lunar month. The Water-Land Ceremony of the Joseon Dynasty continued until the 10th year of King Jungjong's reign (1515) when it was abolished.

These days, the Water-Land Ceremony is held all over Korea as a traditional

Buddhist event that embraces the equality of all beings and expresses respect for life. In addition, the Korean Cultural Heritage Administration announced in 2013 its intent to have the "*Gukhaeng suryuk daejae* (國行水陸大齋; *State-Sponsored Water-Land Great Ceremony*)" designated as an Intangible Cultural Heritage. The Jogye Order welcomed it, saying, "Unlike other ceremonies of Buddhism, the Water-Land Ceremony embraces all life without discrimination, and thus, serves the common good."

수륙재(水陸齋)

수륙재는 물이나 육지에서 방황하는 원혼과 아귀에게 음식을 공양하여 그들을 천도하는 의식이다. 수륙재는 양나라 무제(502~549) 때 시작했다고 알려지고 있다. 불심이 두터웠던 무제는 유주무주의 고혼들을 구제하는 일이 제일가는 공덕이라 여겨 지공화상에게 〈수륙재의문(水陸齋儀文)〉을 짓게 하고 505년 강소성 금산사(金山寺)에서 재를 베풀었다. 송나라에 들어와서는 〈수륙재의문〉이 새롭게 보급되며 전국적으로 성행했다. 우리나라에서는 처음으로 고려 태조 23년(940) 12월에 수륙재가 시작되었다. 이후 광종 21년(970)에 수원 갈양사에 수륙도량을 개설했다. 일연의 제자였던 혼구는 〈신편수륙의문(新編水陸儀文)〉을 지어 수륙재를 더욱 성행하게 했다. 조선을 개국한 태조는 1397년 진관사에 59칸의 수륙사를 건립하고 고려 왕씨들을 위한 수륙재를 베풀었다. 이후 매년 2월과 10월 보름날에 국가 행사로 수륙재를 성대하게 열었다. 태종 15년(1415)부터는 날짜를 1월 15일로 바꾸어 시행하였다. 조선의 수륙재는 중종 10년(1515)까지 시행되다가 결국 폐지됐다. 현대에도 수륙재는 만물평등과 생명존중 사상을 담고 있는 불교의 전통 행사로서 널리 행해지고 있다. 더하여 2013년 문화재청은 동해 삼화사와 서울 진관사의 국행수륙대재(國行水陸大齋)를 중요무형문화재로 지정 예고하였다. 조계종에서는 이를 환영하며 "다른 재들과 달리 모든 생명을 차별 없이 아우르는 수륙재는 매우 사회적이며 공익적인 성격을 가지고 있다"고 의미를 설명했다.

Fill in the Blanks

❖ 1. "*Suryuk-jae*" is a memorial ceremony to placate vengeful spirits wandering on the land or in water and _____ _____. (아귀)

❖ 2. The Water-Land Ceremony is said to have begun during the _____ of Emperor Wu (무제) of the Liang Dynasty. (재위)

❖ 3. He thought that saving the spirits of the deceased who had no one to offer _____ for them, would accrue the foremost merit. (제사)

❖ 4. In Song Dynasty, the *Text for the Water-Land Ceremony* enjoyed _____ popularity and was practiced nationwide. (새로운)

❖ 5. In 1397, King Taejo established a Water-Land Ceremony Building (수륙사) which had a total area of 59 _____. (칸)

❖ 6. There he held the ceremony to _____ the spirits of the Wang clan, the royal family of the former Goryeo Dynasty. (달래다)

❖ 7. Afterward, King Taejo held magnificent _____ ceremonies biannually. (국가가 후원하는)

❖ 8. Beginning from 1415, the ceremony was offered once a year on the 15th day of the ___ _____ _____. (음력 정월)

❖ 9. The Water-Land Ceremony of the Joseon Dynasty continued until the 10th year of King Jungjong's reign (1515) when it was _____. (폐지되다)

❖ 10. These days, the Water-Land Ceremony is held all over Korea as a traditional Buddhist event that embraces the _____ of all beings and expresses _____ for life. (평등, 존중)

Questions

1. To whom is the Water-Land Ceremony offered?
2. When did the Water-Land Ceremony begin in China?
3. When was the first Water-Land Ceremony held in Korea?
4. Why did Joseon's King Taejo offer elaborate Water-Land Ceremonies?
5. When was the intent to designate the Water-Land Ceremony as an Intangible Cultural Heritage announced?

Unit 3

Yeongsan-jae (靈山齋)

Yeongsan-jae is a Buddhist ceremony that reenacts the Buddha's teaching of the *Lotus Sutra* on Vulture Peak in India 2,600 years ago. The purpose of the *Yeongsan-jae* is to deliver both the living and the dead from suffering to happiness. Thus, *Yeongsan-jae* is not simply a performance but a solemn Buddhist ritual in which all those present participate.

In addition, the proceedings of *Yeongsan-jae* have elements of traditional culture in terms of music, dance, and drama. In particular, the Buddhist music known as *beompae* (verses sung in praise of the Buddha and his teachings) and *Hwacheong* (songs of well-wishing) is believed to have greatly influenced Korea's traditional folk music. *Yeongsan-jae* is performed annually at Bongwon-sa Temple in Seoul. It is Korea's Intangible Cultural Heritage No. 50 and also inscribed on UNESCO's Intangible Cultural Heritage List.

It is not clear when the *Yeongsan-jae* was first performed. However, from the fact that *Beompae*, one element of *Yeongsan-jae*, is referenced in *Samguk yusa* (*Legends and History of Korea's Three Kingdoms*), as well as in the inscription on the stele of National Preceptor Jingam at Ssanggye-sa Temple, we can deduce that *Yeongsan-jae* was already being performed during the Silla era. In addition, from the section titled "Wolmyeong sajo (月明師條)" in *Samguk yusa* and in *Joseon geumseok chongnam* (朝鮮金石總覽; *Comprehensive Survey of Joseon Epigraphy*), we know that Buddhist ceremonies to console the spirits of the deceased, also the objective of *Yeongsan-jae*, existed during the Silla era.

영산재(靈山齋)

영산재는 지금으로부터 약 2,600년 전 인도 영취산에서 석가모니 부처님이 여러 중생이 모인 가운데《법화경》을 설하실 때의 모습을 재현한 불교의식이다. 영산재는 산 자와 죽은 자가 다함께 고통을 벗어나 행복에 이르게 하는 데 의미가 있다. 따라서 영산재는 단순한 공연이 아니라 대중이 함께 참여하는 장엄한 불교의식이다. 또한 영산재는 의식의 절차가 음악, 무용, 연극 등 전통문화의 요소를 내포하고 있다. 특히 범패, 화청 등의 불교음악이 우리 전통적인 민속음악 등에 큰 영향을 끼친 것으로 사료된다. 해마다 서울 봉원사에서 거행되는 영산재는 대한민국 중요무형문화재 제50호이며 유네스코 세계무형문화유산이기도 하다.

영산재가 처음 행해졌던 시기는 확실하지 않으나 영산재를 구성하는 기본 요소 중 하나인 범패가《삼국유사》및 쌍계사에 있는 진감국사 비명에 기록되어 있는 것으로 보아 신라시대에 이미 행하여졌던 것임을 알 수 있다. 또 영산재의 목적이 되는 천도 등의 불교 의례도 이미 신라 시대부터 있었음이《삼국유사》의 '월명사조(月明師條)'나《조선금석총람(朝鮮金石總覽)》등을 통해서 알 수 있다.

Fill in the Blanks

❖ 1. *Yeongsan-jae* is a Buddhist ceremony that reenacts the Buddha's teaching of the _____ _____ on Vulture Peak. (법화경)

❖ 2. Thus, *Yeongsan-jae* is not simply a performance but a _____ Buddhist ritual in which all those present participate. (장엄한)

❖ 3. In addition, the _____ of *Yeongsan-jae* have elements of traditional culture in terms of music, dance, and drama. (절차)

❖ 4. *Yeongsan-jae* is performed _____ at Bongwon-sa Temple in Seoul. (해마다)

❖ 5. It is Korea's _____ Cultural Heritage No. 50 (무형)

❖ 6. It is also _____ UNESCO's Intangible Cultural Heritage List. (등재되다)

❖ 7. It is not _____ when the *Yeongsan-jae* was first performed. (확실한)

❖ 8. *Samguk yusa* (_____ and History of Korea's Three Kingdoms) (설화)

❖ 9. In the inscription on the _____ of National Preceptor Jingam at Ssanggye-sa Temple (비)

❖ 10. We can _____ that *Yeongsan-jae* was already being performed during the Silla era. (추측하다)

Questions

1. What does *Yeongsan-jae* reenact?
2. What's the purpose of *Yeongsan-jae*?
3. Where is *Yeongsan-jae* presented annually?
4. Is *Yeongsan-jae* believed to have been performed during the Silla era?
5. Is *Yeongsan-jae* inscribed on the UNESCO World Heritage list?

Unit 4

Yesu-jae (豫修齋)

Yesu-jae is a ceremony offered while one is still living in order to pray for a rebirth in the Pure Land after death. In other words, it is offered for the living to be reborn in a better realm among the six possible realms of rebirth. The ceremony is also called "*Saengjeon Yesu-jae*" or "*Saengchil-jae*." Korean temples usually perform *Yesu-jae* in the leap month which occurs once every four years. Buddhism established *Yesu-jae* by incorporating Daoist belief in the Ten Kings of the Dark Realm (十王信仰). *Yesu-jae* is also closely related to faith in Ksitigarbha Bodhisattva.

To prepare for *Yesu-jae*, one first erects an altar in the center of the Dharma hall for the three bodies of the Buddha (三身佛檀): Vairocana, Amitabha, and Sakyamuni Buddha. To the east, an altar for Ksitigarbha Bodhisattva is erected and to the west, an altar for the guardian deities. Outside the Dharma hall, an altar for the Ten Kings of the Dark Realm (冥府十王壇) is erected. This arrangement of altars represents the belief system of esoteric Buddhism. The *Ksitigarbha Sūtra* offers the following explanation.

> When a man dies without having cultivated goodness,
> Having only committed bad deeds during his life,
> Even if his family performs meritorious deeds for his sake,
> He can receive only one-seventh of those merits
> And the rest go to his family, the living.
> Therefore, beings of the present and the future
> Must cultivate goodness for themselves to receive merit.

▶▶ 예수재(豫修齋)

'생전예수재' 또는 '생칠재'라고도 불리는 예수재는 사후 세계에 '극락왕생'을 하기 위하여 살아생전 올리는 재이다. 즉 죽어서 다시 태어날 때 육도의 세계 중에서 좋은 곳에 태어나기 위해서 지내는 재이다. 사찰에서는 일반적으로 4년에 한 번씩 돌아오는 윤달에 예수재를 거행한다. 예수재는 중국 도교의 '시왕신앙(十王信仰)'에서 수용되었으며 지장신앙과도 관련이 깊다.

재를 지낼 때는 삼신불단(三身佛壇)을 법당 안에 설치하고 동쪽에 지장단, 서쪽에 신중단, 법당 밖에는 명부시왕단(冥府十王壇)을 설치한다. 이와 같은 각단의 배열은 밀교적 신앙 구조를 나타낸 것으로 《지장경》에서는 다음과 같이 그 의미를 설명하고 있다.

> 생전에 좋은 인연을 닦지 않고 죄만 많이 지은 사람이 죽은 후,
> 죽은 자의 권속들이 그 사람을 위해 공덕을 베풀지라도,
> 그가 받을 수 있는 것은 7분의 1뿐이고
> 나머지 7분의 6은 살아 있는 사람들 스스로에게 돌아가게 된다.
> 그러므로 현재나 미래의 중생들은 스스로 수행하여 그 공덕을 받으라.

Fill in the Blanks

❖ 1. *Yesu-jae* is a ceremony offered while one is still _____ in order to pray for a rebirth in the Pure Land after death. (살아 있는)

❖ 2. It is offered for the living to be reborn in a better realm among the _____ possible _____ of rebirth. (육도)

❖ 3. Korean temples usually perform *Yesu-jae* in the _____ _____ which occurs once every four years. (윤달)

❖ 4. Buddhism established *Yesu-jae* by incorporating _____ belief in the Ten Kings of the Dark Realm. (도교의)

❖ 5. *Yesu-jae* is also closely _____ _____ faith in Ksitigarbha Bodhisattva. (관련되어 있다)

❖ 6. To prepare for *Yesu-jae*, one first _____ an altar in the center of the Dharma hall for the three bodies of the Buddha. (설치하다)

❖ 7. This arrangement of altars represents the belief system of _____ _____. (밀교)

Questions

1. What is the purpose of *Yesu-jae*?
2. When do Korean temples usually perform *Yesu-jae*?
3. Does *Yesu-jae* have an element of Daoism?
4. Which scripture is most relevant to *Yesu-jae*?
5. Where is the altar for Ksitigarbha Bodhisattva erected during *Yesu-jae*?

Farewell

– Gyeongheo Seongu

I wanted to write you a poem
before you depart on your long journey,
But the tears flow before I could begin.
A man's hundred years is like a traveler's inn;
In the end, which direction my hometown lies in?
Pieces of cloud come out of mountain caves,
The sun sets at the edge of the long rivers.
Though we try to hold onto man's works,
From a distance, everything is sorrow.

송별
 – 경허성우(鏡虛惺牛, 1849~1912)

贈別

멀리 떠나는 그대에게 시를 주어 보내려니	爲君賦遠遊
눈물이 먼저 앞서는구나	使我涕先流
사람살이 백 년이 여관 같거니	百歲如逆旅
끝내 내 고향이 그 어디인고	何方竟首邱
먼 산굴에서 조각 구름 나오고	片雲生遠岫
긴 물가에 지는 해가 내리네	落日下長洲
인간의 일을 손꼽아 세어보나니	屬持人間事
아득해라 모두가 시름뿐이네	悠悠總是愁

Chapter 3

Eminent Monks of Korea
한국의 고승

Unit 1

Wonhyo (元曉)

Wonhyo (617~686), an eminent monk of the Silla era, still holds great appeal in contemporary Korean society due to his fervent wish to attain freedom, a freedom he exemplified in his life. His philosophy, called "the harmonization of doctrinal disagreements (和諍; *hwajaeng*), had great influence on Tang China and Japan. Wonhyo contributed to transforming "aristocratic Buddhism," which focused on the royal family, into a "people's Buddhism."

Wonhyo tried to go to Tang China in 650, together with Uisang, but they did not make it. In 661, at the age of 45, he and Uisang attempted to go to China again. On their way, they were slowed down by days of rain. One day they slept in an earthen shrine, and the next day they took shelter in a tomb. They went to sleep, but not even halfway through the night, ghosts suddenly appeared, and they couldn't sleep any more. Wonhyo stood up to leave when he suddenly experienced a great insight.

> It is because a mind arises that myriad dharmas arise
> It is because a mind subsides that the shrine and the tomb are no different.
> ⋯ (Part omitted) ⋯
> Outside the mind there are no dharmas,
> There is no use in searching elsewhere.
> I will not go to Tang.

After experiencing true Dharma in this way, Wonhyo returned to Silla. With renewed energy he immersed himself in writing books and edifying the people. He left behind many works amounting to 240 titles, including: *Exposition of the Vajrasamādhi Sūtra* (金剛三昧經論; *Geumgang sammae gyeongnon*) and *Commentary on the Awakening of Mahayana Faith* (大乘起信論疏; *Daeseung gisillon so*). In the latter work, Wonhyo comments on the "One Mind (一心)" as follows.

> As all dharmas, whether of purity or pollution, are no different in their true nature, the two gates of truth and falsehood are also no different; hence they are "One (一)." This non-duality is the true nature of all dharmas, and is not void, but our true nature believes and understands this; hence it is called "Mind (心)." However, if they are already not two, how could they become "One?" If "One" has never existed, what is referred to by the term "Mind?" This principle is beyond words and unconnected to thought. As it is difficult to name it precisely, it is called, by constraint, "One Mind."

원효(元曉)

신라의 고승 원효(617~686)는 그가 추구했던 마음의 세계와 자신의 삶으로 표현했던 자유에의 열망으로 인해 오늘날의 우리들에게도 각별한 의미로 다가오는 스님이다. '화쟁사상(和諍思想)'을 통하여 당나라, 일본 등에도 큰 영향을 미쳤던 원효는 왕실 중심의 귀족화된 불교를 민중불교로 바꾸는데 크게 공헌하였다.

원효는 650년 의상과 함께 당나라 유학을 떠났지만 결국 실패하였다. 두 번째로 의상과 함께 당나라 유학을 떠난 것은 45세(661년) 때였다. 길을 가던 중 장마를 만났는데 하루는 땅막[土龕]에서 자고 하루는 무덤[鬼鄕]에서 잤다. 자다가 동티(지신의 노여움)를 만나 마음이 뒤숭숭해서 잠을 잘 수가 없었다. 그리고 곧바로 자리를 박차고 일어난 그에게 커다란 인식의 전환이 일어났다.

마음이 일어나므로 갖가지 현상이 일어나고
마음이 사라지므로 땅막과 무덤이 둘이 아님을
… (중략) …
마음 밖에 법이 없는데

어찌 따로 법을 구하겠는가.

나는 당나라에 가지 않겠다.

이렇게 참된 법을 체험하고 돌아온 그는 이전과는 다른 에너지로 저술과 교화에 힘썼다. 그의 저술은 《금강삼매경론(金剛三昧經論)》과 《대승기신론소(大乘起信論疏)》를 비롯하여 240여 권이라는 방대한 규모이다. 《대승기신론소》에서 원효는 일심(一心)에 대해 다음과 같이 말한다.

염정(染淨)의 모든 법은 그 본성이 둘이 없어, 진망(眞妄)의 이문(二門)이 다름이 있을 수 없기 때문에 '일(一)'이라 이름하며, 이 둘이 없는 곳이 모든 법 중의 실체인지라 허공과 같지 아니하여 본성이 스스로 신해(神解)하기 때문에 '심(心)'이라고 이름한 것이다. 그러나 이미 둘이 없는데 어떻게 '일(一)'이 될 수 있는가? '일(一)'도 있는 바가 없는데 무엇을 '심(心)'이라 말하는가? 이러한 도리는 말을 여의고 생각을 끊은 것이니 무엇이라고 지목할지를 모르겠으나, 억지로 이름 붙여 일심이라 하는 것이다.

Fill in the Blanks

❖ 1. Wonhyo still holds great appeal in contemporary Korean society due to his _____ _____ to attain freedom. (열망)

❖ 2. His philosophy, called "the _____ of doctrinal disagreements" (화쟁)

❖ 3. Wonhyo contributed to transforming "_____ Buddhism," which focused on the royal family, into a "people's Buddhism." (귀족의)

❖ 4. In 661 he and Uisang _____ to go to China again. (시도하다)

❖ 5. One day they slept in an _____ _____, and the next day they took shelter in a tomb. (땅막)

❖ 6. Wonhyo stood up to leave when he suddenly experienced a great _____. (통찰지)

❖ 7. It is because a mind _____ that myriad dharmas arise. (일어나다)

❖ 8. It is because a mind _____ that the shrine and the tomb are no different. (사라지다)

❖ 9. _____ the mind there are no dharmas. (밖에)

❖ 10. There is no use in _____ elsewhere. I will not go to Tang. (찾다)

❖ 11. With renewed energy he _____ himself in writing books and edifying the people. (힘쓰다)

❖ 12. He _____ _____ many works amounting to 240 titles. (남기다)

❖ 13. As all dharmas, whether of purity or _____, are no different in their true nature (오염, 더러움)

❖ 14. The two gates of truth and _____ are also no different. (거짓)

❖ 15. This _____ is the true nature of all dharmas, and is not void. (둘이 아닌 도리)

❖ 16. If "One" has never existed, what is referred to by the _____ "Mind?" (말, 용어)

❖ 17. This principle is beyond words and _____ to thought. (연결되지 않은)

❖ 18. As it is difficult to name it precisely, it is called, _____ _____, "One Mind." (억지로)

Questions

1. Was Wonhyo a monk of the Baekje Kingdom?

2. What does *hwajaeng* mean?

3. Did Wonhyo advocate aristocratic Buddhism?

4. Did Wonhyo try to go to China once?

5. Where did Wonhyo sleep when he experienced a great insight?

Unit 2

Uisang (義湘)

Uisang (625-702) was an eminent monk during the Unified Silla era. Originally of the royal family, he tried with Wonhyo to go to Tang China to study in 650 when he was 25 years old, but this venture failed. In 661, after Wonhyo decided to turn back, Uisang went to China alone at the age of 37 and became a disciple of Master Zhiyan (智儼; 602-668). There he studied with Fazang, who would later greatly consolidate Avataṃsaka thought, and Uisang himself came to realize the profound meaning of Avataṃsaka. Uisang returned to Silla in 670.

Uisang is said to have met Avalokitesvara Bodhisattva during his 100-day prayer in the Avalokitesvara Cave at Naksan-sa Temple. Based on this experience, he wrote *Baekhwa doryang barwonmun* (白花道場發願文; *Vow Made at White Flower Enlightenment Site*). Through this short vow, consisting of 200 Chinese characters, Uisang conveyed his aspiration which may be summarized as follows: "I aspire to honor Avalokitesvara as my teacher, life after life, to be reborn instantly in the realm of White Flower Enlightenment, to learn the perfect Dharma and to attain insight into the non-arising of all existences."

In 676, under royal decree, Uisang established Buseok-sa Temple on Mt. Taebaeksan in Yeongju. He began to teach the doctrine of the Avataṃsaka School and eventually attracted over 3,000 students, making Buseok-sa a center of Avataṃsaka studies. Soon Uisang became the founder of Korea's Hwaeom School. If Wonhyo exerted himself in edification, research, and writing, Uisang contributed to educating students and enhancing the religious order.

Gatha on the Dharma Nature (法性偈; *Beopseong ge*), one of Uisang's major works, consists of 210 Chinese characters. It is a masterpiece steeped with profound insight into Avataṃsaka thought.

Gatha on Dharma Nature

Dharma nature is perfectly interfused with no trace of duality.
All dharmas are unmoving and originally quiescent.
No name, no form; all distinctions are severed
It is known only through the wisdom of enlightenment, not by any other way.

True nature is extremely profound and supremely subtle.
It maintains no self-nature but manifests according to conditions.
Within One there is All, and within Many there is One.
One is identical to All, and Many are identical to One.

A minute particle of dust contains the ten directions
As do all particles of dust.
An immeasurably long *kalpa* is identical to a single moment of thought,
A single moment of thought is identical to an immeasurably long *kalpa*.

The nine eras and the ten eras are mutually identical;
Yet they are not in confusion but function separately

The moment one arouses the aspiration for enlightenment, it is attained.
Samsara and nirvana are always in harmony.
Principle and phenomena lack real distinctions,
This is the world of the ten Buddhas and Samantabhadra Bodhisattva.

Entering into the Buddha's "ocean seal samādhi,"
Inconceivable Dharma talks are given at will endlessly.
A Dharma rain of jewels that benefits living beings fills all space,
Living beings benefit according to their capacity to understand.

Therefore, when the practitioner returns to his original source,
He cannot obtain it without severing all deluded thoughts.
Commanding unconditional wholesome skill under perfect control,
He returns home and is endowed according to his capacity.

With an inexhaustible treasure of *dharanis* and Dharma talks
He adorns the dharma realm— the palace of genuine jewels.
Finally, seated on the throne of the Middle Way of Ultimate Reality,
From times long past he has not moved—hence his name is Buddha.

의상(義湘)

의상(625~702)은 통일신라시대 중기의 왕족 출신 고승이다. 26세였던 650년 원효와 함께 당에 유학길을 떠났으나 실패하였다. 다시 37세이던 661년 당에 유학하여 지엄(至嚴)삼장의 문하에서 화엄의 대성자인 법장과 함께 수학하여 화엄의 깊은 뜻을 깨달은 후 670년 귀국하였다.

의상은 낙산사 관음굴에서 벽일기도를 하던 중 관세음보살을 친견하였다고 한다. 이로부터 그의 저서인 〈백화도량발원문(白花道場發願文)〉이 나온다. 200자 정도의 단문인 이 발원문에서 의상은 "세세생생 관세음으로 스승 삼기를 바라며, 한 찰나 사이에 백화도량에 왕생하여 정법을 듣고 무생법인을 증득케 하여지이다"고 발원한다.

의상은 676년에 왕의 뜻을 받아 영주 태백산에서 부석사를 창건하고 화엄교학을 강술하였다. 그러자 3,000여 제자가 운집하여 부석사는 화엄학의 중심지가 되었다. 이윽고 의상은 한국 화엄종의 시조가 되었다. 원효가 교화, 연구, 저술에 힘썼다면 의상은 후진 교육과 교단향상에 크게 이바지하였다고 할 수 있다.

의상의 대표작인 《법성게》는 210자의 게송으로 화엄사상의 깊은 뜻을 나타낸 명작이다.

법의 본성 원융하여 두 모습이 본래 없고	法性圓融無二相
모든 법은 부동하여 본래부터 고요하며	諸法不動本來寂
이름 없고 모습 없어 그 모두가 끊겼으니	無名無相絶一切
깨달아야 아는 자리 다른 경계 아니로다.	證智所知非餘境
그대로의 참성품은 매우 깊고 미묘하며	眞性甚深極微妙
자기 본성 못 지키고 인연 따라 생겨나니	不守自性隨緣成

하나 속에 일체 있고 일체 속에 하나 있어　　一中一切多中一
하나가 바로 일체이고 일체가 바로 하나로다.　一卽一切多卽一

그 하나의 티끌 속에 시방세계 들어있고　　　一微塵中含十方
일체 모든 티끌마다 또한 역시 그러하니　　　一切塵中亦如是
한량없는 긴 세월이 바로 일념 찰나이고　　　無量遠劫卽一念
한 찰나의 한 생각이 바로 무량 세월일세.　　一念卽是無量劫

구세십세 서로 얽혀 상즉하고 있는데도　　　九世十世互相卽
어지럽지 아니하고 따로따로 뚜렷하네.　　　仍不雜亂膈別成

처음 발심 내는 때에 문득 정각 이루나니　　初發心時便正覺
생과 사와 열반 모두 서로 함께 있지만은　　生死涅槃相共和
이와 사인 본체 현상 아득하여 분별없어　　理事冥然無分別
시방제불 보현보살 대인들의 경계로다.　　　十佛普賢大人境

부처님의 해인삼매 선정 속에 계시면서　　　能人海印三昧中
부사의한 무진법문 마음대로 쏟아내니　　　繁出如意不思議
중생 위한 보배 법비 온 누리에 가득하여　　雨寶益生滿虛空
중생들이 그릇 따라 모든 이익 얻는구나.　　衆生隨器得利益

그러므로 수행자가 근본자리 돌아갈 땐　　　是故行者還本際
번뇌망상 끊지 않곤 증득할 수 없음이며　　叵息妄想必不得
연 없는 좋은 방편 마음대로 잡아 쓰며　　　無緣善巧捉如意
본고장에 돌아가니 분수 따른 각을 얻네.　　歸家隨分得資糧

다라니의 다함없는 법문진리 보배로써　　　以陀羅尼無盡寶
일법계를 장엄하여 보배궁전 만들고서　　　莊嚴法界實寶殿
궁극으로 실상자리 중도상에 앉고 보니　　窮坐實際中道床
예로부터 제자린데 이름하여 부처라네.　　　舊來不動名爲佛

Fill in the Blanks

❖ 1. In 661, after Wonhyo decided to _____ _____, Uisang went to China alone and became a disciple of Master Zhiyan. (되돌아오다)

❖ 2. There he studied with Fazang, and Uisang himself came to realize the _____ _____ of Avataṃsaka. (깊은 뜻)

❖ 3. Uisang is said to have met _____ Bodhisattva during his 100-day prayer in the Avalokitesvara Cave at Naksan-sa Temple. (관음)

❖ 4. I aspire to _____ Avalokitesvara as my teacher, life after life. (모시다)

❖ 5. I aspire to attain insight into the _____ of all existences. (무생)

❖ 6. In 676, under _____ _____, Uisang established Buseok-sa Temple on Mt. Taebaeksan in Yeongju. (왕명)

❖ 7. He began to teach the _____ of the Avataṃsaka School and eventually attracted over 3,000 students. (교리)

❖ 8. Soon Uisang became the _____ of Korea's Hwaeom School. (설립자)

❖ 9. _____ on the Dharma Nature (법성게 法性偈; Beopseong ge)

❖ 10. Dharma nature is perfectly _____ with no trace of duality. (원융하다)

❖ 11. All dharmas are _____ and originally quiescent. (부동한)

❖ 12. It maintains no self-nature but manifests according to _____. (인연)

❖ 13. Within One there is _____, and within Many there is One. (일체)

❖ 14. A minute particle of _____ contains the ten directions. (티끌)

❖ 15. An immeasurably long *kalpa* is identical to a single _____ of thought. (찰나)

❖ 16. _____ and nirvana are always in harmony. (생사)

❖ 17. Principle and _____ lack real distinctions. (사)

❖ 18. Entering into the Buddha's "_____ _____ samādhi" (해인)

❖ 19. Living beings benefit according to their _____ to understand. (근기)

❖ 20. Therefore, when the practitioner returns to his _____ _____, (근본 자리)

❖ 21. He cannot obtain it without severing all _____ thoughts. (미혹된)

❖ 22. With an inexhaustible treasure of dharanis and Dharma talks, he adorns the _____ _____. (법계)

Questions

1. Was Uisang a member of royalty before he entered the monastic order?
2. Who were Uisang's primary teacher in China?
3. How long did Uisang offer prayers in the Avalokitesvara Cave at Naksan-sa Temple?
4. What is the name of the temple Uisang established by royal decree?
5. How many students did Uisang attract when he taught the doctrine of Avataṃsaka?

Unit 3

Jinul (知訥)

The Goryeo era monk Bojo Jinul (普照知訥; 1158~1210) liked to call himself "Ox-Herder (牧牛子; Moguja)." King Huijong bestowed on him the posthumous title, National Preceptor Buril Bojo (佛日普照國師), which literally means "a state teacher whose wisdom illuminates universally like the Buddha-sun."

The Jogye Order regards National Preceptor Do-ui Wonjeok (道義元寂) as its founder and National Preceptor Bojo Jinul (普照知訥) as an ancestor who developed the order. Jinul wanted to reform the order and establish temples as a venue for Seon practice. He also put a priority on resolving the conflicts between the Seon School and the Doctrinal School.

In 1190 (the 20th year of King Myeongjong's reign), Jinul organized a practice community and issued the *Declaration of Concentration-Wisdom Community* (定慧結社文). The Concentration-Wisdom Community cultivated both concentration and wisdom with renewed determination. It was a movement to restore the true Dharma by putting an end to secularized Buddhism which pursued such things as protection of the state or personal fortune. It was also a movement to revive practice-centered Buddhism which walked the true supra-mundane path. In addition, it was also a movement to transform Buddhism from an "aristocratic Buddhism" to a "people's Buddhism" and thus to renew and reinvigorate it. It is said that hundreds of members of the royalty and the nobility joined this movement.

Around 1200, Jinul taught at Gilsang-sa on Mt. Songgwangsan for 11 years, and students flocked there from all corners of Korea. He guided many people to cultivate a more solid faith by teaching them three types of practice. First, he taught them the "balanced maintenance of alertness and calmness" (惺寂等持門); second, faith and understanding according to the "complete and sudden teaching" (圓頓信解門); third, "the shortcut approach [to enlightenment]" (徑截門) by observing the *hwadu*. Jinul integrated the Seon and Doctrinal Schools by emphasizing that there are no Buddhas other than sentient beings.

Jinul wrote many books, including: *Straight Talk on the True Mind* (眞心直說; *Jinsim jikseol*), *Secrets on Cultivating the Mind* (修心訣; *Susim gyeol*), *Declaration of the Concentration-Wisdom Community* (定慧結社文; *Jeonghye gyeolsa mun*), and *Treatise on the Complete and Sudden Attainment of Buddhahood* (圓頓成佛論; *Wondon seongbullon*). In *Susim gyeol*, he says:

> The three worlds are ablaze in affliction, like a house on fire. How can you bear to tarry here and complacently endure such ongoing suffering? If you wish to avoid wandering in samsara, there is no better way than to seek Buddhahood. If you want to become a Buddha, understand that the Buddha is the mind, so how can you search for the mind in the far distance? It is not outside your body. The physical body is an illusion, for it is subject to birth and death; the true mind is like space, uninterrupted and immutable.

지눌(知訥)

고려의 스님 지눌(1158~1210)은 평소 스스로를 '소를 치는 사람(牧牛子)'이라 부르기를 즐겼으며, 입적 후 희종으로부터 '부처님의 해처럼 널리 비추는 나라의 스승[佛日普照國師]'이라는 시호를 받았다.

대한불교조계종에서는 도의국사를 조계종의 종조로 여기고, 보조국사 지눌을 조계종의 중천조(重闡祖)로 여기고 있다. 지눌은 당시 불교계의 승풍을 개혁하여 사찰을 수행 도량으로 정립시킴과 동시에 선·교의 갈등을 해소하는 것을 자신의 과제로 삼았다.

1190년(명종 20년) 지눌은 수행을 위해 모인 단체인 결사를 조직하면서 〈정혜결사문(定慧結社文)〉을 선포하였다. 정혜결사는 선정과 지혜를 함께 닦는 결사이다. 정혜결사는 당시에 극히 세속화된 '호국·기복불교'에서 '정법불교'로의 복귀운동이며, 진실한 출세간의 길을 밟는 '수행불교'의 재건운동이며, 퇴폐하고 변질되어 버린 '궁중불교'에서 참신하고 생명 있는 '대중불교'로 변화하는 운동이었다. 당시 왕족·귀족으로서 이 결사에 가입한 사람만 해도 수백 명에 달했다 한다.

1200년 지눌이 송광산 길상사에서 11년 동안 제자들을 가르칠 때 사방에서 사람들이 몰려들었다. 지눌은 성적등지문(惺寂等持門), 원돈신해문(圓頓信解門), 경절문(徑截門)의 3개 문을 통해 수행을 이끌었는데, 이를 통해 믿음에 들어가는 자가 많았다. 지눌은 중생을 떠나 부처가 따로 없음을 강조하여 선종과 교종을 통합하였다. 저서로《진심직설(眞心直說)》,《수심결(修心訣)》,《정혜결사문(定慧結社文)》,《원돈성불론(圓頓成佛論)》등이 있다. 그는《수심결》에서 다음과 같이 말하고 있다.

삼계(三界)의 뜨거운 번뇌가 마치 불타는 집과 같은데, 어찌하여 그대로 머물러 긴 고통을 달게 받을 것인가. 윤회를 벗어나려면 부처를 찾는 것 보다 더한 것이 없다. 부처란 곧 이 마음인데 마음을 어찌 먼 데서 찾으려고 하는가. 마음은 이 몸을 떠나 따로 있는 것이 아니다. 육신은 헛것이어서 생이 있고 멸이 있지만, 참마음은 허공과 같아서 끊어지지도 않고 변하지도 않는다.

Fill in the Blanks

❖ 1. Bojo Jinul liked to call himself "_____ (목우자).

❖ 2. King Huijong bestowed on him the _____ _____, National Preceptor Buril Bojo. (시호)

❖ 3. Jinul wanted to _____ the order and establish temples as a venue for Seon practice. (개혁하다)

❖ 4. He also put a priority on resolving the _____ between the Seon School and the Doctrinal School. (갈등)

❖ 5. In 1190 Jinul organized a _____ _____ and issued the *Declaration of Concentration-Wisdom Community*. (결사)

❖ 6. It was a movement to restore the true Dharma by putting an end to _____ Buddhism. (속화된)

❖ 7. It was also a movement to revive _____ Buddhism which walked the true supra-mundane path. (수행 중심의)

❖ 8. In addition, it was also a movement to transform Buddhism from an "aristocratic Buddhism" to a "_____ _____." (대중불교)

❖ 9. Students _____ there from all corners of Korea. (찾아들다)

❖ 10. First, he taught them the "balanced maintenance of _____ and calmness." (성성함)

❖ 11. He taught them faith and understanding according to the "_____ ____ _____ teaching." (원돈신해문)

❖ 12. Third, the _____ approach [to enlightenment] by observing the *hwadu* (지름길)

❖ 13. Jinul integrated the Seon and Doctrinal Schools by emphasizing that there are no Buddhas _____ _____ sentient beings. (떠나서)

❖ 14. The three worlds are _____ in affliction, like a house on fire. (불타는)

❖ 15. If you wish to avoid wandering in samsara, there is no better way than to_____ Buddhahood. (구하다)

❖ 16. Understand that the Buddha is the _____. (마음)

❖ 17. So how can you search for the mind in the _____ _____? (멀리서)

❖ 18. The physical body is an _____, for it is subject to birth and death (헛것)

❖ 19. The true mind is like _____, uninterrupted and immutable. (허공)

Questions

1. Did Jinul use the name "Buril Bojo" during his life?
2. What does Moguja mean?
3. Is Jinul regarded as the founder of the Jogye Order?
4. What is the name of the practice community Jinul organized in 1190?
5. Of the three types of practice Jinul taught, what is the third one called?

Unit 4

Iryeon (一然)

National Preceptor Bogak Iryeon (普覺一然; 1206~1289) was a monk during the reign of Goryeo King Chungnyeol. He received the full precepts at the age of 14 from Ven. Dae-ung (大雄) at Jinjeon-sa on Mt. Seoraksan, a temple of the Gajisan Seon School. He passed the state examination for Buddhist monks in 1227 at age 22. In 1237, when he was 32 years old, he attained enlightenment while investigating the following *hwadu*: "The realm of sentient beings doesn't decrease, nor does the realm of Buddhas increase." Iryeon learned the structure of Ganhwa Seon, which was basically introduced by Jinul and revived by Hyesim, but he also embraced the Seon thought of other Buddhist lineages extensively.

In 1256, he began to compile the *Augmented Five Positions of Caoshan and Dongshan* (重編曹洞五位; *Jungpyeon jodong owi*) at Gilsang-am Hermitage in Namhae and published it in 1260. Beginning in 1249, Iryeon also participated in a 10-year project to make ink rubbings of the *Goryeo daejanggyeong*. From 1277 until 1281, he resided at Unmun-sa in Cheongdo, honoring the decree of King Chungnyeol, where he extensively revived the Seon tradition. At that time the king bestowed on him the title "National Preceptor." It is also at the time when he is thought to have begun writing *Samguk yusa* (三國遺事; *Legends and History of the Korea's Three Kingdoms*).

Samguk yusa reflects Iryeon's Buddhist thought, best summarized as a humanistic affection for sentient beings and a belief in equality. The book also gives us insight into the lives of slaves, some of whom even became Buddhist monks. *Samguk yusa* also contains 14 *Hyangga*, poems written in the archaic native writing system. These also reveal Iryeon's affection for the common people. Choe Namseon highly praised the *Samguk yusa* by saying, "If I had to choose between *Samguk sagi* (三國史記) and *Samguk yusa* (三國遺事), I'd definitely choose the latter." It is fortunate that all extant editions of *Samguk yusa* were eventually designated as either Korean National Treasures or Korean Treasures, since they had previously been underappreciated in their status as cultural heritage. Following is an excerpt from the sayings of Iryeon:

> The great Way of the ancients is like this; you should keep and preserve it well. The essence of genuine phenomena and images is like diamond; it is neither changed nor destroyed. You should know that Buddhas are also like this. A mind reflects another mind like a mirror placed in front of another mirror; a light merges with another light, and thus, they never oppose each other; mind functions naturally in stillness.

일연 (一然)

보각국사 일연(1206~1289)선사는 고려 충렬왕 때의 스님이다. 14세 때 가지산문 계열의 설악산 진전사에서 대웅(大雄)장로에게 구족계를 받았고, 22세인 1227년 승과에 급제하였다.

32세 때인 1237년 포산(包山: 琵瑟山) 묘문암(妙門庵)에 머물면서 "중생 세계는 줄지도 않고 부처 세계는 늘지도 않는다."라는 화두를 참구하다가 크게 깨쳤다. 일연은 기본적으로 지눌이 소개하고 혜심이 크게 발흥시킨 간화선의 사유 체계를 이어받았지만 다른 계통의 선사상도 폭넓게 수용하였다.

1256년에는 남해 길상암에서 《중편조동오위(重編曹洞五位)》를 편집하기 시작하여 1260년에 출간하였다. 1249년부터 약 10여 년 동안 대장경 간행 사업에도 직접 관여하였다. 1277년부터는 충렬왕의 명에 따라 청도 운문사에서 1281년까지 살면서 선풍을 크게 일으켰다. 이때 충렬왕에 의해 국사로 추대되었고 《삼국유사(三國遺事)》를 집필하기 시작한 것으로 추정된다.

《삼국유사》에 투영된 일연의 불교 사상은 중생에 대한 인간적 애착과 평등사상이었다. 책의 곳곳에 노비들의 생활상이 실려 있고 그중에는 출가수행을 하는 노비들도 있다. 또한 14수에 이르는 향가의 채록 사실 역시 민중의 삶에 대한 일연의 애정을 보여준다. 육당(六堂) 최남선(崔南善)은 "《삼국사기(三國史記)》와 《삼국유사》 중에서 하나를 택하여야 될 경우를 가정한다면, 서슴없이 후자를 택할 것"이라며 삼국유사를 높이 평가한 바 있다. 그동안 문화재 지정에서 낮게 평가되었던 《삼국유사(三國遺事)》가 늦게나마 국보 및 보물로 지정되었음은 다행스러운 일이다. 다음은 스님의 말이다.

옛날의 큰 도는 이와 같으니 스스로 잘 지켜 가져라. 실증된 사상(事象)의 체는 금강과 같아서 변하지도 파괴되지도 않는다. 오직 부처도 능히 이와 같음을 알아라. 마음과 마음이 서로 비춤이 마치 거울 앞의 거울과 같아서, 빛과 빛이 서로 융섭하여 각각 거스르지 않으니 어찌 가만히 작용하지 않겠는가?

Fill in the Blanks

❖ 1. He received the _____ _____ at the age of 14 from Ven. Dae-ung (대웅) at Jinjeon-sa on Mt. Seoraksan. (비구계)

❖ 2. He passed the _____ _____ for Buddhist monks in 1227 at age 22. (국가고시)

❖ 3. "The _____ of sentient beings doesn't decrease, nor does the realm of Buddhas increase." (계)

❖ 4. Iryeon also embraced the Seon thought of other Buddhist lineages _____. (널리)

❖ 5. Iryeon also participated in a 10-year project to make _____ _____ of the *Goryeo daejanggyeong*. (인경)

❖ 6. At that time the king bestowed on him the title "_____ _____." (국사)

❖ 7. *Samguk yusa* reflects Iryeon's Buddhist thought, best _____ as a humanistic affection for sentient beings and a belief in equality. (요약되다)

❖ 8. "If I had to choose between *Samguk sagi* (삼국사기) and *Samguk yusa* (삼국유사), I'd definitely choose the _____." (후자)

❖ 9. It is fortunate that all _____ editions of *Samguk yusa* were eventually designated as either Korean National Treasures or Korean Treasures. (현존하는)

❖ 10. The _____ of genuine phenomena and images is like diamond. (체)

❖ 11. It is neither changed nor _____. (파괴되다)

❖ 12. A mind _____ another mind like a mirror placed in front of another mirror. (비추다)

❖ 13. A light merges with another light, and thus, they never _____ each other. (거스르다)

❖ 14. Mind functions naturally in _____. (고요)

Questions

1. Was Jinjeon-sa the home temple of Iryeon?
2. Of Korea's nine Seon Schools, which school did Jinjeon-sa belong to?
3. How old was Iryeon when he passed the state examination for Buddhist monks?
4. Did Iryeon practice Ganhwa Seon?
5. Where did he begin to write *Samguk yusa*?
6. What two Buddhist concepts are reflected in Iryeon's *Samguk yusa*?

Unit 5

Taego Bou (太古普愚)

Taego Bou (太古普愚; 1301~1382), one of the most important Seon masters of the late Goryeo era, is regarded as the ancestor who revived the Jogye Order of Korean Buddhism. There are three reasons for this assessment. First, he integrated the nine Korean Seon Schools, collectively called "Gusan Seonmun (九山禪門)," while at the same time, extensively publicizing the five Doctrinal Schools. In this way he revived a holistic, universal Buddhism, now a distinctive characteristic of Korean Buddhism. Second, he firmly established the practice of Ganhwa Seon. Third, the Buddhist tradition formulated by Bou was the precursor to the Jogye Order of today.

Bou began his monastic life at the age of 13 at Hoe-am-sa Temple in Yangju under the guidance of Seon Master Gwangji. He began to investigate *hwadu* at the age of 19 but strived at doctrinal studies as well. He passed the state examination for monks, called "Hwa-eom Seon (華嚴選)," at age 26, and then began investigating the *hwadu* "Mu (無)," which had originally come from Zhaozhou. He attained great enlightenment at dawn on the seventh day of the first lunar month of 1338 when he was 38 years old.

Bou embarked on a journey to Yuan China in 1346 at the age of 46 to meet with Seon Master Shiwu Qinggong (石屋清拱, 1257~1352). In the seventh month of the next year, he met Master Shiwu, and the two masters polished their understanding of Dharma with each other. Bou remained for 40 more days and studied the tradition of Linji Seon from Master Shiwu. In 1348, he returned to Korea carrying the robe and bowl of the Yangqi Line of the Linji School that Master Shiwu had presented to him. He later established the thought and practice of Ganhwa Seon, which he had learned from the Linji School, into Goryeo Buddhism.

When King Gongmin asked Bou how he should rule the country, he answered: "The sacred and benevolent mind is the foundation of edification and governance. Thus, turn your own light in upon yourself."

Bou's writings include the *Analects of Seon Master Taego* (太古和尙語錄; *Taego-hwasang-eorok*) and the *Posthumous Words of Taego* (太古遺音; *Taego yueum*). Following is part of the "*Song of Taegoam Hermitage*" (太古菴歌; *Taegoam-ga*), which Bou wrote when he lived for five years at Taegoam, located on Mt. Bukhansan.

> I reside in this hermitage, but none knows me.
> So deep and so secluded, but there are no barriers.
> It contains and covers heaven and earth, with no front or back,
> And is not located in the east, west, north or south.
>
> Set all aside and do not arouse false thoughts.
> This then is the Buddha's great enlightenment.
> Eons and eons ago, I exited the door.
> For a brief moment I am staying on this road.

태고보우(太古普愚)

고려 말을 대표하는 선승 보우스님(1301~1382)은 대한불교조계종의 중흥조로 여겨진다. 그 이유는 첫째, 당시 분열되어 있던 구산선문(九山禪門)을 포섭하고 오교(五敎)를 널리 홍보하여 원융회통적인 한국 불교의 전통을 중흥하였고, 둘째, 간화선 수행 체계를 확고히 정착시켰고, 셋째, 보우를 중심으로 형성된 법통이 조계종의 주류를 형성하였기 때문이다.

보우는 13세에 가지산문의 법맥을 이은 양주 회암사에서 광지선사에게 출가했다. 19세부터 화두를 참구하며 수행하면서도 교학에도 매진하여 26세에 승과인 화엄선(華嚴選)에 합격하였다. 이후 조주선사의 무자(無字) 화두를 참구하던 중 38세(1338년) 되던 해 정월 7일 새벽에 대오하였다.

46세(1346년)되던 해 보우는 중국의 석옥청공(石屋淸珙, 1257~1352)선사를 친견하기 위해 원나라로 향한다. 이듬해 7월 석옥선사를 만나 서로의 깨달음을 탁마하고는, 40여 일 동안 선사의 곁에서 임제선을 공부하였다. 그리고 이듬해인 1348년 석옥선사로부터 전해 받은 임제종 양기파의 의발을 휴대하고 귀국하였다. 이후 임제선 계통의 간화선 사상과 수행체계를 고려 불교에 정착시켰다.

또한 공민왕이 초빙하여 나라를 다스리는 일을 물었을 때에는 "거룩하고 인자한 마음이 모든 교화의 근본이요 다스림의 근원이니, 빛을 돌이켜 마음을 비추어 보라"고 하였다.

저서로《태고화상어록(太古和尚語錄)》과《태고유음(太古遺音)》이 있다. 다음은 스님이 북한산에 태고암을 짓고 5년 동안 지낼 때 쓴〈태고암가〉이다.

내가 사는 이 암자 나도 몰라라.
그윽하고 깊지만 막힘이 없네.
건곤을 모두 가두어 앞뒤가 없고
동서남북 어디에도 머물지 않네.

놓아버려라 망상 피우지 말라.
이는 곧 부처의 큰 깨달음이니
내 일찍 오랜 옛적 이 문을 나왔으니
지금 잠시 이 길에 머물고 있네.

Fill in the Blanks

❖ 1. Taego Bou is regarded as the ancestor who _____ the Jogye Order of Korean Buddhism. (중흥하다)

❖ 2. First, he _____ the nine Korean Seon Schools, collectively called "Gusan Seonmun." (통합하다)

❖ 3. Second, he _____ established the practice of Ganhwa Seon. (확고히)

❖ 4. Third, the Buddhist tradition formulated by Bou was the _____ to the Jogye Order of today. (선도자)

❖ 5. He began to investigate hwadu at the age of 19 but strived at _____ _____ as well. (교학)

❖ 6. Bou _____ on a journey to Yuan China in 1346 at the age of 46 to meet with Seon Master Shiwu Qinggong. (떠나다)

❖ 7. The two masters _____ their understanding of Dharma with each other. (탁마하다)

- 8. Bou remained for 40 more days and studied the tradition of _____ Seon from Master Shiwu. (임제)
- 9. In 1348, he returned to Korea carrying the _____ and _____ of the Yangqi Line of the Linji School. (의발)
- 10. When King Gongmin asked Bou how he should _____ the country, he answered (다스리다)
- 11. "The sacred and benevolent mind is the foundation of edification and governance. Thus, _____ your own light in upon yourself." (회, 돌리다)
- 12. I reside in this _____, but none knows me. (암자)
- 13. So deep and so secluded, but there are no _____. (막힘)
- 14. Set all aside and do not arouse _____ _____. (망상)
- 15. _____ and eons ago, I exited the door. (오랜 옛적)

Questions

1. Was Taego Bou a monk of the Silla era?
2. How does the Jogye Order view Bou?
3. From which *hwadu* did Bou attain enlightenment?
4. Who did Bou meet when he went to Yuan China?
5. What did Bou carry with him when he returned from China?

Unit 6 — Seosan Hyujeong (西山休靜)

Seosan Hyujeong (西山休靜: 1520~1604) was an eminent monk of the mid-Joseon era and a monk general who, in 1592, led a volunteer band of monk soldiers to fight the invading Japanese troops during the Imjin War. His other Dharma name is Cheongheo (清虛). He was the 63rd Patriarch in the Seon lineage of Korean Buddhism.

From the age of 12, he studied Confucian classics and martial arts at Seonggyungwan National Confucian Academy for three years. At age 15, he traveled to many temples on Mt. Jirisan with his friends, receiving great inspiration from the Buddha-Dharma upon hearing the talk of Great Master Yeonggwan. From then on, he delved into Buddhist sutras for three years, after which he entered the Buddhist order under the guidance of Ven. Sung-in (崇仁長老). He then concentrated on study and practice. One day he was passing by a village named Yeokseongchon and heard the cry of a cock at midday. At that instant, he attained sudden enlightenment on the nature of mind.

In 1549 (the 4th year of King Myeongjong's reign), when he was 30 years old, he passed the state examination for monks, which had been temporarily revived by Ven. Bou. He received the highest score and was appointed as Head of the Seon and Doctrinal Schools (禪教兩宗判事). In 1557, at age 37, he resigned from this post on the pretext that serving as head of the Seon and Doctrinal Schools was not the original duty of a monk. After that, he resided on Mt. Myohyangsan for a long while.

At the outbreak of the Imjin War in 1592, Seosan organized a monk army with his disciple, Samyeong, and fought against the Japanese invaders. He expounded a solid philosophy on the concept of nation by saying that religions have no national borders, but religious believers do. After an audience with King Seonjo at Uiju, Seosan proposed that all weak or crippled monks should remain at their temples and offer prayers to protect Korea while he would organize a monastic militia with the other monks to expel the enemy. In this way he became the "Overall Supervisor of the Seon and Doctrinal Schools from the Sixteen Lineages in the Eight Provinces." He then led about 5,000 monk soldiers into battles. After helping defend the nation, he and the king returned to Hanyang, the capital of the Joseon Dynasty. Thanks to the many activities of Master Seosan, the status of Joseon Buddhism rose in the eyes of many Koreans.

Seosan wrote *Seonga gwigam* (禪家龜鑑; *The Mirror of Seon*) to awaken Buddhists who were feeling oppressed by Confucianism and to convey to them the essence of Seon. The first edition was carved onto printing woodblocks in Chinese, the language he wrote it in. It was later published at many places in Korea, in Chinese as well as in Korean. The book later became very well known and was praised as a masterpiece not just in Korea but also in both China and Japan.

Seosan had more than 1,000 students. There were four major disciples who passed on Seosan's teachings, but each of them eventually established their own distinctive lineages. They were: Samyeong Yujeong (四溟惟政), Pyeonyang Eongi (鞭羊彥機), Soyo Taeneung (逍遙太能), and Jeonggwan Ilseon (靜觀一禪). In addition to *Seonga gwigam*, Seosan's writings include: the *Collected Works of Venerable Cheongheo* (清虛堂集; *Cheongheo dangjip*), *Seongyo seok* (禪教釋; *Explanation of Seon and Doctrine*) and *Seongyo gyeol* (禪教訣; *Resolution of [the Differences between] Seon and Doctrine*). Following is an excerpt from *Seonga gwigam*.

> The [direct] transmission of the mind by the World Honored One (Buddha) at three different locales is the gist of Seon; what was spoken by him in his lifetime is the gate of Doctrine. Therefore, it is said, "Seon is the Buddha mind; Doctrine is the Buddha word."
>
> To cultivate meditation while harboring lust in your heart is like steaming sand to make cooked rice; if you cultivate meditation

but take a life, that is like blocking your ears when shouting; if you cultivate meditation but commit theft, that is like trying to fill a leaking goblet; if you cultivate meditation but tell lies, that is like trying to make incense out of feces. Even though you may have much wisdom, all of these acts constitute the Way of the mara.

▶▶ 서산휴정(西山休靜)

휴정(1520~1604)은 조선 중기의 고승이며 임진왜란 때 의승군을 이끈 승장이다. 호는 청허(淸虛)·서산(西山)이며, 한국 불교의 선맥에서 제63대 조사이다.

12세 때 성균관에서 3년 동안 글과 무예를 익혔다. 과거를 보았으나 뜻대로 되지 않자, 15세에 친구들과 지리산의 여러 사찰을 유력하던 중에 영관대사의 설법을 듣고 불법에 감응을 하였다. 이후 3년 간 경전을 깊이 탐구하던 중 깨달은 바가 있어 숭인장로(崇仁長老)를 스승으로 모시고 출가하였다. 이후 공부에만 전념하던 어느 날 역성촌이란 마을을 지나다가 한 낮에 닭 우는 소리를 듣고 문득 마음자리를 깨달았다.

30세(1549년, 명종 4년)되던 해에 보우스님에 의하여 잠시 부활했던 승과에 최고 득점으로 급제하였고, 선교양종판사(禪敎兩宗判事)가 되었다. 37세(1557년) 되던 해 선교양종판사직이 승려의 본분이 아니라며 자리에서 물러나 묘향산에서 오래 주석하였다.

1592년 임진왜란이 일어나자 서산대사는 제자인 사명대사 등과 함께 승군을 조직하여 왜병에 맞서 싸웠다. 종교에는 국경이 없으나 신앙인에게는 조국이 있다는 확고한 민족 철학을 제시했던 것이다. 의주에서 선조를 뵌 서산대사는 전국의 스님들 중 노약자는 절에 남아 나라를 지키는 기도를 하게하고 나머지 스님들로는 의승군을 조직하여 적군을 몰아내겠다고 했다. 그리하여 8도(道) 16종(宗) 도총섭(都摠攝)이 된 서산대사는 의승 5천 명을 모집하여 인솔하고 전선으로 갔다. 관군을 도와 나라를 지킨 후에는 왕을 모시고 한양으로 돌아왔다. 서산대사의 이런 활동으로 조선시대 불교의 실질적 위치가 격상될 수 있었다.

서산대사는 유교에 눌려있는 불교인들을 일깨우기 위해서《선가귀감(禪家龜鑑)》을 집필하여 선지(禪旨)를 제시했다. 초판은 1579년 원문인 한문본으로 판각되었다. 그 뒤 여러 곳에서 한문본과 언해본으로 간행되었고 중국과 일본에서도 널리 알려진 명저로 꼽히는 책이 되었다.

스님은 제자가 1천여 명에 이르렀다. 서산의 법을 이은 가장 대표적인 제자는 사명 유정, 편양언기, 소요태능, 정관일선으로 청허 문하의 4대 문파를 이루었다. 저서로는《선가귀감》외에도《청허당집(淸虛堂集)》,《선교석(禪敎釋)》,《선교결(禪敎訣)》등이 있다. 다음은《선가귀감》에서 가려 뽑은 것이다.

세존께서 세 곳에서 마음을 전하신 것(三處傳心)은 선지(禪旨)가 되고, 한평생 말씀하신 것은 교문(敎門)이 되었다. 그러므로 선은 부처님의 마음이고, 교(敎)는 부처님의 말씀이다.

음란하면서 참선을 하는 것은 모래를 쪄서 밥을 지으려는 것과 같고, 살생하면서 참선하는 것은 자신의 귀를 막고 소리를 지르는 것과 같고, 도둑질하면서 참선하는 것은 밑 빠진 그릇에 물이 가득 차기를 바라는 것과 같고, 거짓말을 하면서 참선하는 것은 똥으로 향을 만들려는 것과 같다. 이런 것들은 비록 많은 지혜가 있더라도 모두 악마의 길을 이룰 뿐이다.

Fill in the Blanks

❖ 1. Seosan Hyujeong was also a _____ _____ who led a volunteer band of monk soldiers to fight the invading Japanese troops. (승장)

❖ 2. He was the 63rd Patriarch in the _____ _____ of Korean Buddhism. (선맥)

❖ 3. He studied Confucian _____ and martial arts at Seonggyungwan National Confucian Academy for three years. (고전)

❖ 4. From then on, he _____ _____ Buddhist sutras for three years, after which he entered the Buddhist order. (파고들다)

❖ 5. One day he was passing by a village named Yeokseongchon and heard the cry of a cock at _____. (한낮)

❖ 6. At that instant, he attained sudden enlightenment on the _____ ___ _____. (마음자리)

❖ 7. He resigned from this post on the _____ that serving as head of the Seon and Doctrinal Schools was not the original duty of a monk. (명분)

❖ 8. At the _____ of the Imjin War in 1592, Seosan organized a monk army with his disciple, Samyeong. (발발)

❖ 9. He expounded a solid philosophy on the concept of nation by saying that religions have no national borders, but _____ _____ do. (종교인)

❖ 10. After an _____ with King Seonjo at Uiju (알현)

❖ 11. Seosan proposed that all weak or _____ monks should remain at their temples and offer prayers to protect Korea. (지체장애가 있는)

❖ 12. He would organize a _____ _____ with the other monks to expel the enemy. (의승군)

❖ 13. Seosan wrote *Seonga gwigam* to awaken Buddhists who were feeling _____ by Confucianism and to convey to them the essence of Seon. (눌리다)

❖ 14. The book later became very well known and was praised as a _____ not just in Korea but also in both China and Japan. (명작)

❖ 15. The [direct] transmission of the mind by the World Honored One (Buddha) at three different _____ is the gist of Seon. (장소)

❖ 16. To cultivate meditation while harboring lust in your heart is like _____ sand to make cooked rice. (찌다)

❖ 17. If you cultivate meditation but take a life, that is like _____ your ears when shouting. (막다)

❖ 18. If you cultivate meditation but commit theft, that is like trying to fill a _____ goblet. (새는)

Questions

1. In which war did Seosan act as a monk general?
2. Unusual for a monk, Seosan also studied at the National Confucian Academy. How old was he when he entered this school?
3. Where did Seosan have a profound encounter with Buddhism?
4. What prompted him to attain enlightenment?
5. What is Seosan's masterful writing that was also popular in China and Japan?

Unit 7

Gyeongheo Seongu (鏡虛惺牛)

Gyeongheo Seongu (鏡虛惺牛; 1840~1912) was a 12th generation descendant of Cheongheo Hyujeong (aka. Seosan Hyujeong). In the late Joseon era, Seon Dharma was so weakened that it had been almost in a state of hibernation for about 100 years. Gyeongheo revived the Seon Dharma in this dark era and reinvigorated the Seon lineage; hence he is called the ancestor who revived Korea's modern Seon.

Beginning with organizing a practice community at Haein-sa in 1899, Gyeongheo restored Seon centers at major Korean temples and took the initiative in re-establishing Seon practice. Thanks to his efforts, the Seon tradition, which had first appeared in Korea in the late Silla era, began to reappear. This revived and strengthened Korean Buddhism enough to endure the oppression of Japanese Buddhism during the upcoming 36 years of Japanese occupation.

In addition, Gyeongheo compiled *Seonmun chwaryo* (禪門撮要; The *Essential Sayings of the Seon House*). This contains essential analects and commentaries he selected from both Chinese and Korean Seon traditions in order to guide Seon practitioners. For information on the life and works of Gyeongheo, there are two versions of the *Collected Works of Gyeongheo* (鏡虛集; *Gyeongheo jip*), one edited and prefaced by Ven. Hanam, and the other by Ven. Manhae.

At age 23, Gyeongheo was appointed as a lecturer at Donghak-sa's scriptural study center, eventually attracting 1,000 students from all parts of Korea. He was unsurpassed as a lecturer. In 1879 (the 16th year of King Gojong's reign), when he was 31 years old, he attained great enlightenment upon hearing the words, "The cow has no nostrils."

Throughout his life, Gyeongheo explored how to adapt Buddhism to daily life. He constantly promulgated Seon doctrine, not only through Dharma talks but also in daily conversation or in questions and answers sessions.

Even his way of speaking and his sometimes unusual actions were teaching expedients he had gleaned from his Seon practice. Most Seon monastics of contemporary Korean Buddhism have either directly inherited his Seon lineage or been indirectly influenced by him.

Gyeongheo sometimes lived in villages, but he never owned a house. He has never been an abbot either, a position usually taken by senior monks. He truly lived a life of non-possession. Following is an excerpt from his work, *Verse of Seon Meditation* (參禪曲; *Chamseon gok*):

In meditation, the ancients never wasted even a moment.
Yet I am so slack and so unmindful.
In meditation, the ancients pierced their thighs with awls to remain awake.
Yet I am so slack and so unmindful.
In meditation, the ancients cried in fury at the end of the day
Yet I am so slack and so unmindful.

Intoxicated by consciousness, obscured by ignorance,
My life is passing by, unaware and deluded.
Alas, what a pity! Earnest admonitions are ignored.
Rebukes are not heeded but brushed aside.
How could this deluded mind be led onto the right path?

경허성우(鏡虛惺牛)

경허(1840~1912) 선사는 청허 휴정 선사의 12세손이다. 경허가 살던 조선시대 말에 선법(禪法)이 크게 위축되어 근 백여 년 동안 거의 동면 상태에 있었다. 이러한 때에 이 땅에 다시 선법을 부흥시키고, 실낱같이 이어지던 선맥을 살렸기에 경허는 한국 근대 선의 중흥조로 일컬어진다.

경허는 1899년 해인사 결사를 필두로 전국의 유명한 사찰에 선원을 복원하고 앞장서서 수행을 이끌었다. 이를 통해 신라 후기로부터 면면히 이어져온 선풍이 마침내 재현되기 시작하여 우리 불교가 36년의 강제 점령 기간 동안 일본 불교를 견디어 낼 힘을 내부적으로 축적하기 시작하였다.

또한 우리나라와 중국 불교 선문(禪門)의 중요한 어록과 논을 가려 뽑은《선문촬요(禪門撮要)》를 찬술하여, 수행자들에게 선의 지침을 제공해 주었다. 또한 경허스님에 관한 자료로 한암스님이 저술한《경허집》과 만해스님이 저술한《경허집》이 있다.

선사는 23세 때 동학사 강원의 강사로 추대되어 제방 학인을 지도함에 학인들이 1천까지 이르렀다. 강백으로서 선사를 능가하는 강백은 당대에는 없었다고 한다. 31세 되던 1879년(고종 16년) 선사는 "소가 콧구멍이 없다"는 말에 대오하였다.

그는 전 생애를 통하여 선의 생활화를 모색하였다. 법상에서 행한 설법뿐만 아니라 대화나 문답을 통해서도 언제나 선을 선양하였고, 문자의 표현이나 특이한 행동까지도 선으로 겨냥된 방편이요, 작용이었다. 오늘날 불교계의 선승들 중 대부분은 그의 선풍을 계승하는 문손이거나 간접적인 영향을 받은 사람들이다.

선사는 마을에 살았으나 집을 가진 바 없었으며, 절에서도 그 흔한 주지 한번 해본 적이 없는 무소유의 삶을 살았다. 다음은 경허스님의 〈참선곡〉 중 일부이다.

    예전 사람 참선할 제 마디 그늘 아꼈거늘
    나는 어이 방일하며
    예전 사람 참선할 제 잠 오는 것 성화하여
    송곳으로 찔렀거늘 나는 어이 방일하며
    예전 사람 참선할 제 하루해가 가게 되면
    다리 뻗고 울었거늘 나는 어이 방일한고

    무명업식(無明業識) 독한 술에 혼혼불각(昏昏不覺) 지나가니
    오호라 슬프도다 타일러도 아니 듣고
    꾸짖어도 조심(操心) 않고 심상(尋常)히 지나가니
    혼미한 이 마음을 어이하여 인도할꼬?

Fill in the Blanks

❖ 1. Gyeongheo Seongu was a 12ᵗʰ generation _____ of Cheongheo Hyujeong. (손)

❖ 2. In the late Joseon era, Seon Dharma was so _____ that it had been almost in a state of hibernation for about 100 years. (위축되다)

❖ 3. Gyeongheo revived the Seon Dharma in this _____ _____. (암흑기)

❖ 4. To endure the oppression of Japanese Buddhism during the _____ 36 years of Japanese occupation (다가오는)

❖ 5. There are two _____ of the *Collected Works of Gyeongheo*. (버전)

❖ 6. Gyeongheo was appointed as a _____ at Donghak-sa's scriptural study center. (강사)

❖ 7. He was _____ as a lecturer. (타의 추종을 불허하는)

❖ 8. Throughout his life, Gyeongheo explored how to _____ Buddhism to daily life. (적용하다)

❖ 9. Even his way of speaking and his sometimes unusual actions were teaching _____ he had gleaned from his Seon practice. (방편)

❖ 10. In meditation, the ancients never _____ even a moment. (허비하다)

❖ 11. Yet I am so slack and so _____. (깨어 있지 못한)

❖ 12. In meditation, the ancients pierced their thighs with _____ to remain awake. (송곳)

❖ 13. Earnest _____ are ignored. (타이름)

❖ 14. _____ are not heeded but brushed aside. (꾸짖음)

❖ 15. How could this deluded mind be led onto the _____ _____? (바른 길)

Questions

1. Did Gyeongheo live in the mid-Joseon era?
2. In the late Joseon era, was Seon Dharma vibrant?
3. Who revived the modern Seon of Korea?
4. Who edited *Gyeongheo jip*?
5. How is modern Korean Seon indebted to Gyeongheo?

Unit 8

Manhae (萬海)

Manhae Han Yong-un (韓龍雲; 1879~1944) is a Korean monk who lived in the era of the Korean Empire (1897~1910) and the Japanese colonial period. Working in Buddhism-related journalism and education, Manhae promoted reformation of the inept and uninspired Buddhism of his time and active Buddhist engagement in society.

As one of the 33 nationalist representatives in the March 1st Movement of 1919, Manhae added the "Three Articles of pledges" at the end of the Korean Declaration of Independence, which are deemed valuable even by contemporary standards. Even during his imprisonment, he spoke out for Korea's independence and freedom by writing the "Letter for the Independence of Joseon."

Manhae was a Seon master but was called by many titles, including poet, patriot, teacher, novelist, revolutionary, and radical reformist. He acquired all these titles because he was a central figure in organizing and conducting resistance movement against Japanese oppression while pursuing the development of Buddhism in independent and autonomous ways. In addition, he was able to express his thoughts eloquently in his poetry, novels, and other writings. He was a Buddhist monk walking the path of truth, but at the same time, he firmly stood up for his beliefs by raising the torch of resistance during the dark period of Japanese occupation. That's why he is considered one of the most important figures in modern Korean history.

Manhae was practicing Seon meditation at Geonbong-sa on Mt. Geumgangsan when his teacher, Seon Master Manhwa (萬化), gave him the Dharma name "Manhae (萬海)" in 1917. The name implied that he was "one who could drink the entire ocean in a single sip." Thereafter, he plunged into the ocean of suffering of sentient beings. Manhae's political and social activities are largely divided into three areas: reforming Buddhism, making Buddhism more accessible to the public, and resisting the Japanese.

First, in his efforts to reform Buddhism, he authored the *Joseon bulgyo yusillon* (朝鮮佛教維新論; *Proposal for Revitalizing the Buddhism of Joseon*). Second, to make Buddhism more accessible, he compiled the *Bulgyo daejeon* (佛教大典; *Great Canon of Buddhism*) based on essential passages he selected from the Buddhist canon and reinterpreted into simple, modern language. Third, in resisting the Japanese, he participated in the March 1st Independence Movement. As the "*Thoughts on Joseon's Independence*," a work he authored in prison, reveals, he rejected Japan's colonial policies and engaged in the struggle for Korean liberation.

Immediately after his release from a 3-year prison sentence for his activities in the March 1st Independence Movement, Manhae remarked to a visiting journalist, "I have enjoyed pleasure in hell." In Buddhism, there is one bodhisattva who entered hell voluntarily. That was Samantabhadra Bodhisattva who vowed to be the last to leave hell after helping all people be liberated from it. Manhae spent the last years of his life at a house he called Simujang. The house was blasted by snowstorms in the winter as he had built the house facing north because he didn't want his house to face the Government General of Korea, the headquarters of Japanese colonialism. Following is one of the poems Manhae wrote.

The Silence of Love

Love is gone.
Ah, my love has gone.
Breaking away from me, he has gone on a little path,
splitting the green of the mountains toward the autumnal maple grove.

Our old oath, once solemn and radiant like golden flowers,
is turned to cold dust and blown away on the puff of a breeze.

The memory of our trembling first kiss changed my destiny

and then disappeared, stepping backward.
I was deafened by his sweet voice and blinded by his flower-like face.

Since it is human to love,
I was neither unwary nor unguarded about parting.
Yet, his departure was so sudden
that my startled heart burst into renewed sorrow.
Still, I know that to make this parting a useless source of tears
will only break the spirit of love.
Thus, I transferred the force of my uncontrollable surge of sorrow
and poured it onto the crown of a new hope.

As we worry about parting when we meet,
so do we believe in reunion when parting.
Though my love is gone, I am not parted from him.
The song of love, unable to overcome its melody,
swirls around the silence of love.

만해(萬海)

만해 한용운(韓龍雲, 1879~1944)은 대한제국과 일제 강점기를 산 한국의 스님이다. 불교와 관련된 언론, 교육 등의 활동을 하면서 종래의 무능한 불교 개혁과 현실 참여를 주장하였다. 3·1 만세 운동 당시 민족대표 33인의 한 사람으로서 〈독립선언서〉의 '공약 3장'을 추가 보완하였다. 또한 옥중에서 〈조선 독립의 서(書)〉를 지어 독립과 자유를 주장하였다.

만해 한용운 선사는 선사였을 뿐 아니라, '시인', '애국지사', '독립지사', '선생', '소설가', '시인', '혁명가', '급진적 개혁가' 등 다양한 호칭으로 불리어진다. 이렇게 불리는 것은 무엇보다도 스님이 일본 제국주의의 탄압에 맞서 승려들의 항거와 투쟁을 일으키는 중심적 인물이었으며, 끊임없이 한국 불교의 주체적 발전 방향을 모색한 인물이었기 때문이다. 뿐만 아니라 스님은 그의 사상을 시나 소설로 그리고 저작 등으로 나타내었다. 그는 구도의 길에 들어선 승려인 동시에 일제 암흑기 동안 일관하여 저항의 햇불을 높이 치켜들고 지조를 꿋꿋이 지켜낸 인물이다. 따라서 우리나라 근현대사의 흐름에 있어서 가장 중심이 되는 인물이라고 할 수 있다.

금강산 건봉사에서 참선수행을 하다가 1917년 스승 만화(萬化)선사로부터 '한입으로 온 바다(萬海)를 다 마셨다'고 하여 '만해'라는 법호를 받은 선사였던 그는 다시 중생들의 고해바다로 뛰어들었다. 만해 선사의 정치·사회적 행적은 크게 '불교의 개혁', '불교의 대중화', '항일 민족운동'의 세 부분으로 나눌 수 있다.

첫 번째로 그는 '불교의 개혁'을 위해서《조선불교유신론(朝鮮佛敎維新論)》을 발표하였다. 둘째, '불교의 대중화'를 위해서 불교 경전 중에서 주요한 부분을 선별하여 그것을 평이하게 현대적으로 해석한《불교대전(佛敎大典)》을 편찬하였다. 셋째, '항일 민족운동'의 경우 3·1운동에 실천적으로 참여하였다. 또한 감옥에서 쓴〈조선독립의 감상〉에서 보듯이 그는 식민지 정책을 거부하고 민족 해방을 앞당기는 투쟁을 하였다.

3·1운동으로 3년을 감옥에서 지낸 뒤 출옥한 직후 찾아온 한 기자에게 만해는 "지옥에서 쾌락을 즐겼노라"고 말했다. 불교에선 스스로 지옥에 들어간 이가 있다. 모든 중생을 지옥에서 벗어나게 하고 나서야 마지막으로 지옥문을 나서겠다고 서원한 지장보살이다. 그는 총독부를 향하기 싫다며 북향으로 지어 북풍 눈보라를 자처한 심우장에서 말년을 보냈다.

님의 침묵

님은 갔습니다. 아아 사랑하는 나의 님은 갔습니다.
푸른 산빛을 깨치고 단풍나무 숲을 향하여 난 적은 길을 걸어서,
차마 떨치고 갔습니다.
황금의 꽃같이 굳고 빛나던 옛 맹서는 차디찬 티끌이 되어서,
한숨의 미풍에 날아갔습니다.
날카로운 첫 〈키스〉의 추억은 나의 운명의 지침을 돌려 놓고,
뒷걸음쳐서 사라졌습니다.
나는 향기로운 님의 말소리에 귀먹고 꽃다운 님의 얼굴에 눈멀었습니다.
사랑도 사람의 일이라 만날 때에 미리 떠날 것을 염려하고 경계
하지 아니한 것은 아니지만, 이별은 뜻밖의 일이 되고 놀란 가슴은
새로운 슬픔에 터집니다.
그러나 이별을 쓸데없는 눈물의 원천을 만들고 마는 것은 스스로
사랑을 깨치는 것인 줄 아는 까닭에, 걷잡을 수 없는 슬픔의 힘을
옮겨서 새 희망의 정수박이에 들이부었습니다.
우리는 만날 때에 떠날 것을 염려하는 것과 같이 떠날 때에
다시 만날 것을 믿습니다.
아아 님은 갔지마는 나는 님을 보내지 아니하였습니다.
제 곡조를 못 이기는 사랑의 노래는 님의 침묵을 휩싸고 돕니다.

Fill in the Blanks

❖ 1. Manhae Han Yong-un lived in the era of the _____ _____ and the Japanese colonial period. (대한제국)

❖ 2. Manhae promoted _____ of the inept and uninspired Buddhism of his time. (개혁)

❖ 3. As one of the 33 _____ _____ in the March 1st Movement of 1919 (민족 대표)

❖ 4. Even during his _____, he spoke out for Korea's independence and freedom. (수감)

❖ 5. Manhae was a Seon master but was called by many _____, including poet, patriot, teacher, novelist, revolutionary, and radical reformist. (호칭)

❖ 6. In addition, he was able to express his thoughts _____ in his poetry, novels, and other writings. (유창하게)

❖ 7. He was a Buddhist monk walking the _____ of truth. (길)

❖ 8. He firmly stood up for his beliefs by raising the _____ of resistance during the dark period of Japanese colonialism. (횃불)

❖ 9. His Dharma name "Manhae (만해)" implied that he was "one who could drink the entire ocean in a _____ _____." (한입)

❖ 10. He rejected Japan's colonial _____ and engaged in the struggle for Korean liberation. (정책)

❖ 11. Immediately after his release from a 3-year prison sentence, Manhae remarked to a visiting journalist, "I have enjoyed _____ in hell." (쾌락)

❖ 12. In Buddhism, there is one bodhisattva who entered hell _____. (스스로)

❖ 13. That was Samantabhadra Bodhisattva who _____ to be the last to leave hell after helping all people be liberated from it. (서원하다)

❖ 14. The house was blasted by _____ in the winter as he had built the house facing north. (눈보라)

Questions

1. What are the two things Manhae promoted?
2. Was he one of the 33 nationalists representatives at the March 1st Movement of 1919?
3. How did Manhae contribute to the Korean Declaration of Independence?
4. Why did Manhae's teacher gave him the Dharma name "Manhae?"
5. What did Manhae say to a journalist upon his release from imprisonment?

Unit 9

Toe-ong Seongcheol (退翁性徹)

Toe-ong Seongcheol (退翁性徹; 1912~1993) inspired modern Koreans to live upright and to attain enlightenment with his renowned aphorism, "Mountains are mountains, water is water." He promulgated Korean Buddhism both inwardly and outwardly with his unwavering observance of the precepts and his easy-to-understand Dharma talks. He organized a practice community movement at Bongam-sa together with fellow monks such as Cheongdam (靑潭; 1902~1971), Ja-un (慈雲; 1911~1992), and Wolsan (月山; 1912~1997). Seongcheol practiced seated meditation for eight years without ever lying down to sleep (長坐不臥) at Seongjeon-am Hermitage. He dedicated himself to practice to such a degree that he didn't even leave the mountain temple to attend his own enthronement ceremony as Supreme Patriarch of the Jogye Order.

Seongcheol is also known as a Buddhist thinker who ceaselessly explored ways to establish a proper Seon tradition. In one of his major works, *Seonmun jeongno* (禪門正路; *The Correct Path of Seon*), published in 1981, he pointed out the limitations of the theory of "sudden enlightenment, gradual cultivation." Thereafter, he clarified the philosophical origin of and a practice method based on "sudden enlightenment, sudden cultivation."

Seongcheol received the novice precepts in 1936 at Haein-sa from the Great Patriarch Dongsan (東山慧日, 1860~1965), and the Bodhisattva precepts and full precepts in 1938 from Unbong. He promoted a renewed Seon style in many ways, including the practice community at Bongam-sa where he resided with Cheongdam and resolved to live like a Buddha. In 1967, he became the first Spiritual Patriarch of Haein Chongnim. In 1981, he was enthroned as the 7th Supreme Patriarch of the Jogye Order of Korean Buddhism. However, he seldom appeared in the secular world.

Seongcheol wrote many books, including: *Seonmun jeongno* (禪門正路; *The Correct Path of Seon*), *Lectures on the Essentials for Entering the Way through Sudden Enlightenment* (頓悟入道要門講說; *Dono ipdo yomun gangseol*), and *Hundred-Day Dharma Talks* (百日法門; *Baegil beommun*). Following is a partial citation from the Dharma talk he delivered on the Buddha's Birthday in 1982.

> Take a good look at yourself.
> You are originally Buddha.
> All truths are within you.
> You are originally pure gold.
> The Buddha did not appear in this world to save us.
> He came to teach us that we are originally saved.

퇴옹성철(退翁性徹)

'산은 산, 물은 물'이란 법어로 현대인에게 올바른 삶과 깨달음을 일깨운 성철(1912~1993)스님은 철저한 계행(戒行)과 알기 쉬운 법어로 한국 불교를 대내외적으로 알리는데 공헌하였다. 그는 청담, 자운, 월산스님 등과 함께 봉암사 결사를 일으켰으며 8년간 성전암에서 장좌불와를 하였다. 종정 추대 때도 산문으로 나오지 않을 정도로 평생 수행으로 일관하였다고 전해진다.

스님은 선풍을 바로 세우기 위한 사상적 모색을 끊임없이 펼친 불교 사상가로서도 알려져 있다. 1981년 간행한 대표적 저서인《선문정로》를 통해 돈오점수론의 한계를 지적하였으며 돈오돈수에 입각한 간화선의 사상적 기원과 실천론을 천명하였다.

1936년 해인사에서 동산 대종사에게 사미계를, 1938년 운봉스님에게 보살계·비구계를 받았다. 봉암사에서 청담스님과 함께 수행하면서 불타답게 살자고 결사하는 등 새로운 선풍을 고양시켰다. 1967년 해인총림 초대 방장이 되었고 1981년 대한불교조계종 제7대 종정에 취임하였다. 세속에는 거의 모습을 나타내지 않았다.

저서로《선문정로》,《돈오입도요문강설》,《백일법문》등이 있다. 다음은 성철스님이 종정으로 있었던 1982년〈부처님오신날 기념 법어〉중에서 인용한 것이다.

> 자기를 바로 봅시다. 자기가 본래 부처입니다.
> 모든 진리는 자기 속에 구비되어 있습니다.
> 자기는 본래 순금입니다.
> 부처님은 이 세상을 구원하러 오신 것이 아니요,
> 이 세상이 본래 구원되어 있음을 가르쳐 주러 오셨습니다.

Fill in the Blanks

❖ 1. Toe-ong Seongcheol inspired modern Koreans to live _____. (바르게)

❖ 2. He _____ Korean Buddhism both inwardly and outwardly with his unwavering observance of the precepts. (널리 알리다)

❖ 3. Seongcheol practiced seated meditation for eight years without ever _____ _____ to sleep. (눕기)

❖ 4. He didn't even leave the mountain temple to attend his own enthronement ceremony as _____ _____ of the Jogye Order. (종정)

❖ 5. He is also known as a Buddhist _____ who ceaselessly explored ways to establish a proper Seon tradition. (사상가)

❖ 6. Thereafter, he clarified the philosophical origin of and a practice method based on "_____ _____, sudden cultivation." (돈오)

❖ 7. He seldom appeared in the _____ world. (세속의)

❖ 8. Following is a _____ citation from the Dharma talk he delivered on the Buddha's Birthday in 1982. (일부의)

❖ 9. Take a _____ look at yourself. (잘)

❖ 10. The Buddha came to teach us that we are originally _____. (구원된)

Questions

1. What is one of Seongcheol's renowned aphorisms?
2. Where did he organize a practice community?
3. How long did Seongcheol practice seated meditation without ever lying down to sleep?
4. Did Seongcheol enjoy coming out of the mountains into the secular world?
5. What theory of practice did he expound on in his 1981 publication?

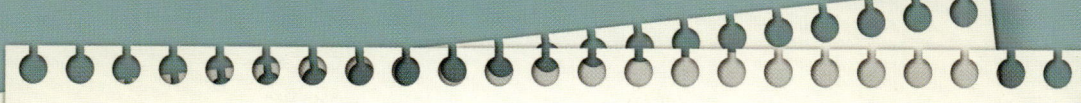

Poem of Enlightenment

– Gyeongheo Seongu

Unexpectedly hearing from a stranger that there is no nostril,
I suddenly realized that the whole universe is my home.
In the June winding roads beneath Yeonam Mountains,
Farmers leisurely give praise with songs of peace.

오도송

- 경허성우

콧구멍이 없다는 사람의 말을 갑자기 듣고
삼천세계가 바로 내 집임을 별안간 깨쳤는데
유월의 연암산 밑의 길이여
들사람은 일이 없어 태평가를 부르네

悟道頌

忽聞人語無鼻孔
頓覺三千是我家
六月鷰岩山下路
野人無事太平歌

Appendix : Answers

문제 해답

Part 2 해답

Chapter 1
The Ethics of Buddhism

1. Ten Unwholesome Deeds (十惡業; *Sibageop*) ...100

• Fill in the Blanks

1. body
2. repent
3. purification
4. life
5. Stealing
6. insult
7. anger
8. misconduct
9. slander
10. covetousness

• Questions

1. Through body, speech, and mind.
2. Speech.
3. No, it is caused by one's mind.
4. Lying, ornate speech, insult, and slander.
5. To the deeds caused by one's mind.

2. The Verse of the Common Teaching of the Seven Buddhas ...103

• Fill in the Blanks

1. scriptures(sutras)
2. cultivate
3. exert
4. afflictions
5. attachment
6. perspective
7. foolish
8. places
9. practice
10. cleansing

• Questions

1. Yes, it is.
2. It refers to the three basic afflictions of greed, anger, and ignorance.
3. No, it doesn't.
4. Because of its concern with putting things into practice.
5. Yes, they do.

3. The *Uposatha* (布薩; *Posal*) ...106

• Fill in the Blanks

1. *uposatha*
2. monastics
3. repents
4. violation
5. based on
6. intervals
7. mutual trust
8. confess
9. mindset
10. generosity

• Questions

1. Twice a month.
2. Three times.
3. To help monastics maintain a life based on precepts without forgetting them.
4. No, it isn't.
5. Courage, loving-kindness, and generosity

4. The *Pavāraṇā* (自恣; *Jaja*) ...108

• **Fill in the Blanks**

1. meditation retreat
2. any wrong
3. once
4. beneficial, bad feelings
5. concern, blame
6. humble mind
7. confrontational

• **Questions**

1. At the end of meditation retreats.
2. Once a year.
3. With humble mind and without anger or bad feelings.
4. You should speak with compassionate mind, without any feeling of confrontation by dividing "you" and "I."

5. Repentance (懺悔; *Chamhoe*) ...110

• **Fill in the Blanks**

1. change
2. signal
3. desires
4. wholeheartedly
5. expiation
6. vanishes
7. conceal
8. trifle
9. hindrance
10. wrongs

• **Questions**

1. Yes, it does.
2. No, it also involves understanding the root cause of the wrongs and not repeating the same wrongs again.
3. No, there aren't. All wrongs can be expiated if one genuinely repent.
4. No, only with repentance they vanish.
5. Without repentance, all the wrongs accumulate to pose a big hindrance to smooth practice.

6. The Three Refuges (三歸依戒; *Samgwi-uigye*), the Five Precepts (五戒; *Ogye*), the Ten Precepts (十戒; *Sipgye*), and Precepts for Bhikkhus and Bhikkhunis ...112

• **Fill in the Blanks**

1. Three Jewels
2. belief
3. vow
4. committing to
5. solid
6. fruit
7. foundation
8. grave offenses
9. tolerated
10. defrocked
11. influence
12. novices

• **Questions**

1. To take refuge in the Three Jewels of Buddhism, namely the Buddha, the Dharma, and the Sangha.
2. Because the first step of a Buddhist is to be committed to the three refuges.
3. No, he or she can't.
4. Yes, it is.
5. No, they don't.
6. Because they are prescribed for novice monks and nuns.
7. No, we are not.

Chapter 2
The Teachings from Scriptures and Recorded Sayings of Sages

1. The *Heart Sutra* (般若心經; Skt. *Prajñāpāramitā-hṛdaya*; Kr.*Banyasimgyeong*) ...116

• **Fill in the Blanks**

1. recited

Appendix : Answers   215

2. characters
3. "emptiness"
4. true nature
5. devoid
6. ceaselessly
7. differ from
8. heart
9. negates
10. doctrine

• **Questions**

1. The *Heart Sutra*.
2. There are 260 Chinese characters.
3. Emptiness.
4. No, it doesn't.
5. No, it doesn't.

2. The *Diamond Sutra* (金剛經; Ch. *Jingang jing*; Kr. *Geumgang gyeong*) …119

• **Fill in the Blanks**

1. foundational sutra
2. condensed
3. basic concepts
4. Jetavana Monastery
5. dialogue
6. Huineng
7. dwelling
8. translated into
9. commentaries
10. four-line
11. overcome
12. compared

• **Questions**

1. Because it is the foundational sutra of the order.
2. No, it expresses the basic concepts of Mahayana Buddhism.
3. It was taught at the Jetavana Monastery in Śrāvastī.
4. Between the Buddha and Subhuti.
5. "Let the mind arise without dwelling on anything."
6. Kumārajīva.
7. So that its devotees may recite the same version of *Diamond Sutra*.

3. Verses on the Faith Mind (信心銘; *Xinxin ming*) …123

• **Fill in the Blanks**

1. Patriarch
2. essentials
3. Middle Way
4. Seon School
5. two extremes
6. relative
7. comprehensive
8. marvel at
9. Supreme Way
10. bereft
11. distinction
12. opinions

• **Questions**

1. Because it contains all the essentials of Seon and Doctrine Schools.
2. The Third Patriarch Sengcan.
3. Middle Way.
4. Yes, he did.
5. Hold no opinions for or against anything.

4. Song of Enlightenment (證道歌; *Zhengdaoge*) …126

• **Fill in the Blanks**

1. state
2. truth
3. rhythm
4. confirmed
5. verse
6. masterworks
7. guidance
8. woodblocks
9. carved
10. designated
11. Publishing
12. excerpt

• **Questions**

1. The attainment of enlightenment.
2. Seon Master Yongjia Xuanjue.
3. The Sixth Patriarch.
4. Yes, it does.
5. Yes, it was.

5. The *Mirror of Seon(Zen)* (禪家龜鑑; *Seonga gwigam*) ...129

• **Fill in the Blanks**

1. authored
2. mirror
3. contemporaries
4. deep reflection
5. annotations
6. initiate
7. mediate
8. mind
9. superiority
10. complemented
11. Chinese edition
12. practical

• **Questions**

1. Because he was greatly disappointed at the way his contemporaries learned Buddhism.
2. Yes, he did.
3. Yes, it was.
4. In 1579.
5. Yes, it was.

Chapter 3
Seon Practice of Korea

1. *Instructions for Sitting Seon* (坐禪儀; *Zuochanyi*) ...132

• **Fill in the Blanks**

1. beginner's book
2. Yunmen House
3. abbot
4. revive
5. volume
6. training text
7. principles
8. arouse
9. cultivate
10. liberation
11. worldly involvement
12. stillness
13. Regulate
14. deprived

• **Questions**

1. How to practice Seon.
2. The Yunmen House.
3. At Hongji Seon Center (洪濟禪院) in Hebei Province.
4. Yes, it is the eighth volume.
5. Ven. Beopjeong.

2. Practice of Ganhwa Seon (看話禪) ...136

1) The Three Essentials of Ganhwa Seon

• **Fill in the Blanks**

1. emphasized
2. triangle
3. practice
4. unwavering
5. indignation
6. doubt
7. reveal
8. single day
9. terrapin
10. useless

• **Questions**

1. Master Gaofeng Yuanmiao.
2. Great faith, great fury, and great doubt.
3. Mt. Sumeru.
4. The moment you were about to slash your bitter enemy in half.
5. Enlightenment cannot be attained.

2) *Hwadu* (話頭) and *Gongan* (公案)

• **Fill in the Blanks**

　1. barriers
　2. free from
　3. block
　4. ordinary
　5. sever
　6. extraordinary
　7. West
　8. courtyard
　9. stick
　10. approachable
　11. documents
　12. absolute
　13. opportune conditions
　14. major
　15. *Cliff*

• **Questions**

　1. Yes, it is.
　2. To block all passages of thoughts and discrimination for practitioners.
　3. No, it can only be approachable by extraordinary thinking.
　4. From "official documents of government."
　5. There are as many as 1,700 *gongans*.

3) Implementation of *Manhaeng* (萬行) and Seon Practice

• **Fill in the Blanks**

　1. traveling
　2. earthly situations
　3. learning
　4. virtuous masters
　5. keep in mind
　6. Pertaining to
　7. be with
　8. idle away
　9. forehead
　10. Contemplate
　11. repay
　12. forewarn

• **Questions**

　1. Traveling practice that Seon practitioners embark on after the three-month Seon retreat is finished.
　2. They test themselves if they can practice *hwadu* well or if their minds are unwavering even in the midst of various situations of the world.
　3. Yes, they do.
　4. They should keep in mind that place of learning is everywhere and never let go of *hwadu* practice.
　5. No, it isn't. The emphasis is on visiting another place of learning.

Part 3 해답

Chapter 1
Temple Ceremonies

1. The Dawn Bell Chant ...148

• Fill in the Blanks

1. sounding
2. upon
3. purify
4. reborn
5. spiritual, splendor
6. praise
7. traditional music
8. spread
9. darkness
10. of
11. shatter
12. enlightenment

• Questions

1. Morning Buddhist ceremony.
2. Yes, it is.
3. Upon the end of *Doryangseok*.
4. Because they are similar in terms of rhythm and tune.
5. Yes, they are because they have characteristics of Korean traditional music.

2. *Yebul*, Morning and Evening Buddhist Ceremonies ...150

• Fill in the Blanks

1. homage
2. Buddhists
3. Verse
4. Scents
5. Incense
6. Prostrations
7. nectar-like tea
8. compassion
9. observance
10. knowledge
11. ten directions
12. utmost sincerity
13. always present
14. wisdom
15. action
16. compassion
17. vows
18. ten major disciples
19. entrusted
20. lamp
21. inexhaustible
22. devotion

• Questions

1. No, it also helps cultivating oneself.
2. Twice.
3. Verse of Tea.
4. The sweet scent of our observance of the precepts, of our meditation, of our wisdom, of our liberation, and of the knowledge of our liberation.
5. It wishes that all beings in the universe attain Buddhahood.

3. The Evening Bell Chant ...155

• Fill in the Blanks

1. before
2. expunge
3. arouse
4. attain, salvation
5. Upon hearing

6. awakened
7. delivered

• **Questions**

1. No, it isn't. It is offered before the evening *yebul*.
2. Yes, it does.
3. No, it doesn't.

Chapter 2
Cheondo-jae (薦度齋)

1. *Sasipgu-jae* (49齋), the Forty-Nine Day Ceremony ...158

• **Fill in the Blanks**

1. collectively
2. wandering
3. death
4. reenacts
5. preparation
6. resentment
7. favorable rebirth
8. flux
9. seventh day
10. ritual
11. spirit tablet
12. altar
13. intermediate
14. bathing
15. attached
16. bubbles
17. presiding
18. looks back at
19. depart
20. greets

• **Questions**

1. No, it isn't. It consists of many types of ceremonies.
2. No, they aren't. *Yesu-jae* is offered for the living.
3. Yes, it is.

4. They pray that the deceased remove all attachments to this world and be reborn in the Pure Land.
5. Sending off the spirit.

2. *Suryuk-jae* (水陸齋), the Water-Land Ceremony ...162

• **Fill in the Blanks**

1. hungry ghosts
2. reign
3. sacrifices
4. renewed
5. bays
6. appease
7. state-sponsored
8. 1st lunar month
9. abolished
10. equality, respect

• **Questions**

1. To the vengeful spirits, wandering on the land or in water and hungry ghosts.
2. During the reign of Emperor Wu (武帝) of the Liang Dynasty.
3. In December in the 23rd year of Goryeo King Taejo's reign (940).
4. To appease the deceased of the Wang clan.
5. In 2013.

3. *Yeongsan-jae* (靈山齋) ...165

• **Fill in the Blanks**

1. Lotus Sutra
2. solemn
3. proceedings
4. annually
5. Intangible
6. inscribed on
7. clear
8. Legends
9. stele
10. deduce

- **Questions**

  1. The Buddha's teaching of the *Lotus Sutra* on the Vulture Peak.
  2. To deliver both the living and the dead from suffering to happiness.
  3. At Bongwon-sa Temple in Seoul.
  4. Yes, it is.
  5. No, it isn't.

4. Yesu-jae (豫修齋) …168

- **Fill in the Blanks**

  1. living
  2. six, realms
  3. leap month
  4. Daoist
  5. related to
  6. erects
  7. esoteric Buddhism

- **Questions**

  1. To pray for a rebirth in the Pure Land after death.
  2. In the leap month, which occurs once in four years.
  3. Yes, it does.
  4. Kṣitigarbha Sūtra.
  5. In the east of the Dharma hall.

Chapter 3
Eminent Monks of Korea

1. Wonhyo (元曉) …172

- **Fill in the Blanks**

  1. fervent wish
  2. harmonization
  3. aristocratic
  4. attempted
  5. earthen shrine
  6. insight
  7. arises
  8. subsides
  9. Outside
  10. searching
  11. immersed
  12. left behind
  13. pollution
  14. falsehood
  15. non-duality
  16. term
  17. unconnected
  18. by constraint

- **Questions**

  1. No, he was a monk of the Silla era.
  2. Harmonization of doctrinal disagreements.
  3. No, he didn't. He favored Buddhism for common people.
  4. No, twice.
  5. In a tomb.

2. Uisang (義湘) …176

- **Fill in the Blanks**

  1. turn back
  2. profound meaning
  3. Avalokitesvara
  4. honor
  5. non-arising
  6. royal decree
  7. doctrine
  8. founder
  9. Gatha
  10. interfused
  11. unmoving
  12. conditions
  13. All
  14. dust
  15. moment
  16. Samsara
  17. phenomena
  18. ocean seal
  19. capacity
  20. original source
  21. deluded
  22. dharma realm

• **Questions**

1. Yes, he was.
2. Master Zhiyan.
3. 100 days.
4. Buseok-sa.
5. 3,000 students.

3. Jinul (知訥) …182

• **Fill in the Blanks**

1. Ox-Herder
2. posthumous title
3. reform
4. conflicts
5. practice community
6. secularized
7. practice-centered
8. people's Buddhism
9. flocked
10. alertness
11. complete and sudden
12. shortcut
13. other than
14. ablaze
15. seek
16. mind
17. far distance
18. illusion
19. space

• **Questions**

1. No, he didn't. It was posthumously bestowed.
2. Ox-Herder.
3. No, he is regarded as an ancestor who developed the order.
4. Concentration-Wisdom Community.
5. The shortcut approach [to enlightenment](徑截門) by observing the *hwadu*.

4. Iryeon (一然) …186

• **Fill in the Blanks**

1. full precepts
2. state examination
3. realm
4. extensively
5. ink rubbings
6. National Preceptor
7. summarized
8. latter
9. extant
10. essence
11. destroyed
12. reflects
13. oppose
14. stillness

• **Questions**

1. Yes, it was.
2. Gajisan Seon School.
3. He was 22 years old.
4. Yes, he did.
5. At Unmun-sa in Cheongdo.
6. Humanistic affection for sentient beings and thought of equality.

5. Taego Bou (太古普愚) …190

• **Fill in the Blanks**

1. revived
2. integrated
3. firmly
4. precursor
5. doctrinal studies
6. embarked
7. polished
8. Linji
9. robe, bowl
10. rule
11. turn
12. hermitage
13. barriers
14. false thoughts
15. Eons

• **Questions**

1. No, he was a monk of the Goryeo era.
2. As an ancestor who revived the Jogye Order of Korean Buddhism.
3. The hwadu of "Mu (無)."

4. Master Shiwu Qinggong.
5. The robe and bowl of the Yangqi Line of Linji School that Master Shiwu had transmitted to him.

6. Seosan Hyujeong (西山休靜) …194

• **Fill in the Blanks**

1. monk general
2. Seon lineage
3. classics
4. delved into
5. midday
6. nature of mind
7. pretext
8. outbreak
9. religious believers
10. audience
11. crippled
12. monastic militia
13. oppressed
14. masterpiece
15. locales
16. steaming
17. blocking
18. leaking

• **Questions**

1. The Imjin War.
2. He was 12 years old.
3. When he traveled around Mt. Jirisan.
4. When he heard a cry of a cock at midday while he was passing by a village named Yeokseongchon.
5. *Seonga gwigam.*

7. Gyeongheo Seongu (鏡虛惺牛) …199

• **Fill in the Blanks**

1. descendant
2. weakened
3. dark era
4. upcoming
5. versions
6. lecturer
7. unsurpassed
8. adapt
9. expedients
10. wasted
11. unmindful
12. awls
13. admonitions
14. Rebukes
15. right path

• **Questions**

1. No, he lived in the late Joseon era.
2. No, it was so dwindled that it was almost in the state of hibernation.
3. Gyeongheo.
4. Ven. Hanam and Ven. Manhae.
5. Most Seon monastics of contemporary Korean Buddhism have either directly inherited his Seon lineage or been indirectly influenced by him.

8. Manhae (萬海) …203

• **Fill in the Blanks**

1. Korean Empire
2. reformation
3. nationalist representatives
4. imprisonment
5. titles
6. eloquently
7. path
8. torch
9. single sip
10. policies
11. pleasure
12. voluntarily
13. vowed
14. snowstorms

• **Questions**

1. Reformation of Buddhism and Buddhist engagement in society.
2. Yes, he was.
3. He added the Three Articles of Pledges.
4. Because he thought of Manhae as "one who

could drink the entire ocean in a single sip."
5. "I have enjoyed pleasure in hell."

9. Toe-ong Seongcheol (退翁性徹) ...208

• **Fill in the Blanks**

1. upright
2. promulgated
3. lying down
4. Supreme Patriarch
5. thinker
6. sudden enlightenment
7. secular
8. partial
9. good
10. saved

• **Questions**

1. "Mountains are mountains, water is water."
2. At Bongam-sa.
3. For 8 years.
4. No, he didn't.
5. Sudden enlightenment, sudden cultivation.

Memo

불교영어 중급2

초판 1쇄 펴냄 2014년 3월 3일
초판 2쇄 펴냄 2019년 3월 5일

편찬 대한불교조계종 교육원 불학연구소
집필 · 번역 지엘통번역센터(원장 진우기)
영어 감수 장미정

발행인 정지현
편집인 박주혜
펴낸곳 조계종출판사

사진 한국불교문화사업단

출판등록 제2007-000078호(2007. 4. 27)
주소 서울 종로구 삼봉로 81 두산위브파빌리온 230호
전화 02)720-6107~9 **팩스** 02)733-6708
구입문의 불교전문서점(www.jbbook.co.kr) 02)2031-2070~1

ISBN 979-11-5580-008-9 04740
      978-89-93629-80-4 (전4권)

※ 책값은 뒤표지에 있습니다.
※ 저작권법에 의하여 보호를 받는 저작물이므로 무단으로 복사, 전재하거나 변형하여 사용할 수 없습니다.
※ 조계종출판사의 수익금은 포교 · 교육 기금으로 활용됩니다.